HEAVEN

90 DEVOTIONS FROM
OUR DAILY BREAD

COMPILED BY DAVE BRANON

Discovery House.
from Our Daily Bread Ministries

Discovery House is affiliated with Our Daily Bread Ministries,
Grand Rapids, Michigan.

Requests for permission to quote from this book should be directed to:
Permissions Department, Discovery House, P.O. Box 3566, Grand Rapids, MI 49501, or contact us by e-mail at permissionsdept@dhp.org.

ISBN: 978-1-62707-487-2

Printed in the United States of America
First printing in 2016

CONTENTS

FOREWORD

When a young boy recanted his story about going to heaven and returning to tell about it, many people were disappointed. His story had become a best-selling book, and Christians by the thousands had read it in an attempt to get an early glimpse into our future home.

You can't really blame people for their fascination with his story, can you? After all, if we plan to go somewhere, it's only natural to find out as much as possible about that place ahead of time. Who doesn't study up on a new country before visiting it on vacation or on business?

The problem is that the Bible doesn't give us the kind of information we want about this place Jesus said He has gone ahead of us to prepare. It doesn't give us the details about exactly what we will be doing, what we will look like, what our homes will be like, how we will interact with each other, and a thousand other details.

For as long as there has been *Our Daily Bread*, our writers have searched the Scriptures to give us little peeks into our heavenly home. None of us has any special insight into it—indeed none of our writers who have gone on to heaven have come back to give us any new revelations about it. Imagine the articles Julie Ackerman Link or Richard DeHaan could write now!

However, what we've been able to say about heaven in the devotional booklet has proved to be helpful and encouraging over the years. We have shared about its remarkable beauty. We have written about the apparent immediacy of being with Jesus after we pass from this earth. We have told about what we learn from the apostle John, who actually got a glimpse of the place. We have mentioned the astounding possibilities that will be ours as believers when Jesus ushers in the new heaven and new earth. And most of all, we have penned articles about the unbelievable honor and privilege of worshiping God as we bask in the light of His presence.

That might not make a book like this a bestseller, but we hope it becomes for you a ray of encouragement, a source of hope, and a welcome reminder that the temporary trials of this life are going to be followed by an existence that is beyond our ability to put it into words.

For now, as we await our grand and glorious future, may these pages awaken anew in your heart an anticipation of sharing eternity with God and with all who have put their faith in His Son.

—Dave Branon

READY FOR GLORY

Read: Philippians 1:12-23

Precious in the sight of the LORD is the death of his faithful servants.
—PSALM 116:15

On March 1, 1981, preacher and Bible commentator D. Martyn Lloyd-Jones lay on his deathbed in London. From 1939 to 1968, he had served as the pastor of that city's Westminster Chapel. Now at the end of his life, Lloyd-Jones had lost the ability to speak. Indicating that he did not want any more prayers for his recovery, he wrote on a piece of paper: "Do not hold me back from glory."

Because life is so precious and fragile, it can be hard to let our loved ones go when the time comes for them to depart this earth and go to heaven. Yet God has set a time when He plans to call us home. Psalm 116:15 tells us, "Precious in the sight of the LORD is the death of his faithful servants."

When Paul saw that death was near, he was encouraged by what awaited him in heaven: "Now there is in store for me the crown of righteousness, which the Lord, the righteous Judge, will award to me on that day—and not only to me, but also to all who have longed for his appearing" (2 Timothy 4:8).

No matter where Christians are in life's journey, their ultimate destination is to "be with Christ, which is better by far" (Philippians 1:23). This should give us confidence in facing life's challenges and comfort when other believers leave us for that glorious home Christ has prepared.

—*Dennis Fisher*

"To go to heaven, fully to enjoy God, is infinitely better than the most pleasant accommodations here." —Jonathan Edwards

THOUGHTS OF HEAVEN

Read: Revelation 21:1-5

Look! God's dwelling place is now among the people, and he will dwell with them. They will be his people. —REVELATION 21:3

Cartoonists often depict those who have gone to heaven as white-robed, ghostly forms floating among the clouds or sitting on golden stairs playing harps. What a far cry from the picture we find in the Bible!

In 1 Corinthians 15, we read that our resurrection bodies, although not subject to death, will be real and tangible—not mere apparitions. And Revelation 21:1–5 tells us that God will bring about "a new heaven and a new earth." He will bring down "the city of the living God, the heavenly Jerusalem" (Hebrews 12:22), and set it upon the new earth as the "new Jerusalem." It is described as having streets, walls, gates, and even a river and trees (Revelation 21:12–22:2).

Life in that city will be wonderful, free from all the debilitating effects of sin. There will be no more death, sorrow, mourning, and pain, for God will make "everything new" (Revelation 21:5). But best of all, God himself will come to live among us, making possible a new level of intimacy with Him.

It's difficult to envision such an existence, but what an exciting prospect! It is all possible because of what Jesus did when He died for us on the cross. This should motivate us to worship Him, live godly lives, and tell others how they too can be assured of a glorious future.

—*Herb Vander Lugt*

"We will not be disembodied spirits in the world to come, but redeemed spirits, in redeemed bodies, in a redeemed universe." —R. A. Torrey

A FOREVER HELLO

Read: 2 Corinthians 4:16–5:8

*Now the one who has fashioned us for this this very purpose is God,
who has given us the Spirit as a deposit, guaranteeing what is to come.*
—2 CORINTHIANS 5:5

After a week's vacation with her daughter and four-month-old grandson Oliver, Kathy had to say goodbye until she could see them again. She wrote to me saying, "Sweet reunions like we had make my heart long for heaven. There, we won't have to try to capture memories in our mind. There, we won't have to pray for the time to go slowly and the days to last long. There, our hello will never turn into goodbye. Heaven will be a 'forever hello,' and I can't wait." As a first-time grandma, she wants to be with her grandson Oliver as much as possible! She's thankful for any time she can be with him—and she's thankful for the hope of heaven, where the wonderful moments will never end.

Our good days do seem too short, and our difficult days far too long. But both kinds of days cause us to long for even better days ahead. The apostle Paul said that he and the Corinthians longed to be "clothed instead with our heavenly dwelling, so that what is mortal may be swallowed up by life" (2 Corinthians 5:4). Although the Lord is with us in this life, we cannot see Him face to face. Now we "live by faith, not by sight" (v. 7).

God made us for the very purpose of being near Him always (v. 5). Heaven will be that "forever hello" we all long for.

—*Anne Cetas*

"The sweetness of reunion is the joy of heaven." —Richard Paul Evans, *Lost December*

HEAVENLY COUNTRY

Read: Hebrews 11:8-16

Our citizenship is in heaven. —PHILIPPIANS 3:20

During high school, my closest friend and I took a pair of horses out for an afternoon ride. We slowly roamed through fields of wildflowers and wooded groves. But when we nosed the horses in the direction of the barn, they took off toward home like twin rockets. Our equine friends knew it was time for dinner and a good brushing, and they could hardly wait.

As Christians, our citizenship is in heaven (Philippians 3:20). Yet sometimes our desires tether us to the here and now. We enjoy God's good gifts, but at the same time, the Bible challenges us to focus "on things above" (Colossians 3:2). "Things above" may include the unseen benefits of heaven: God's enduring presence (Revelation 22:3–5), unending rest (Hebrews 4:9), and an everlasting inheritance (1 Peter 1:4).

Recently I read, "Believers desire the heavenly inheritance; and the stronger the faith is, the more fervent [the desire]." Several Old Testament believers who are mentioned in Hebrews 11 had a strong faith in God that enabled them to embrace His promises before receiving them (v. 13). One such promise was heaven. If we too put our faith in God—through Christ—He will give us a desire for that "better country—a heavenly one" (v. 16), which will help us loosen our grip on the things of this world.

—Jennifer Benson Schuldt

"You will not be in heaven two seconds before you cry out, 'Why did I place so much importance on things that were so temporary?' " —Rick Warren, *The Purpose Driven Life*

THE LIGHT OF THE LAMB

Read: Revelation 21:14-27

The city does not need the sun or the moon to shine on it, for the glory of God gives it light, and the Lamb is its lamp. —REVELATION 21:23

For countless generations people have looked to the sun and moon to light the day and the night. Whether illuminating our path or providing the life-giving radiance for fruitful crops and the nutrients our bodies need, the sun and moon are part of God's marvelous provision of light. The book of Genesis tells us that God gave "the greater light to govern the day and the lesser light to govern the night" (1:16).

But someday God will provide a different kind of illumination. Of the eternal heavenly city, John writes, "The city does not need the sun or the moon to shine on it, for the glory of God gives it light, and the Lamb is its lamp" (Revelation 21:23). Interestingly, the word translated *light* here is more accurately rendered *lamp*. Christ in His glorified state will be the spiritual lamp that lights up that joyous new earth.

The Lord Jesus Christ is "the Lamb of God, who takes away the sin of the world!" (John 1:29). He is also the source of spiritual illumination that makes those who follow Him "the light of the world" (Matthew 5:14). But in eternity He will be the Lamp that lights our way (Revelation 21:23). What a thrill it will be one day to live in the light of the Lamb!

—*Dennis Fisher*

"For the Christian, heaven is where Jesus is. We do not need to speculate on what heaven will be like. It is enough to know that we will be forever with Him." —William Barclay

WE'RE SAFE

[God] has given us new birth . . . into an inheritance that can never perish, spoil or fade. This inheritance is kept in heaven for you.
—1 PETER 1:3–4

The United States Bullion Depository in Fort Knox, Kentucky, is a fortified building that stores five thousand tons of gold bullion and other precious items entrusted to the federal government. Fort Knox is protected by a twenty-two-ton door and layers of physical security: alarms, video cameras, minefields, barbed razor wire, electric fences, armed guards, and unmarked Apache helicopters. Based on the level of security, Fort Knox is considered one of the safest places on earth.

As safe as Fort Knox is, there's another place that's safer, and it's filled with something more precious than gold: Heaven holds our gift of eternal life. The apostle Peter encouraged believers in Christ to praise God because we have "a living hope"—a confident expectation that grows and gains strength the more we learn about Jesus (1 Peter 1:3). And our hope is based on the resurrected Christ. His gift of eternal life will never come to ruin as a result of hostile forces. It will never lose its glory or freshness, because God has been keeping and will continue to keep it safe in heaven. No matter what harm may come to us in this life, God is guarding our souls. Our inheritance is safe.

Like a safe within a safe, our salvation is protected by God. We are secure.

—*Marvin Williams*

"I would not give one moment of heaven for all the joy and riches of the world, even if it lasted for thousands and thousands of years." —Martin Luther

HEAVENLY PERSPECTIVE

Read: 2 Corinthians 4:16–18

What is seen is temporary, but what is unseen is eternal.
—2 CORINTHIANS 4:18

Fanny Crosby lost her sight as an infant. Yet she went on to become one of the most well-known lyricists of Christian hymns. During her long life, she wrote more than nine thousand hymns. Among them are such enduring favorites as "Blessed Assurance" and "To God Be the Glory."

Some people felt sorry for her. A well-intentioned preacher told her, "I think it is a great pity that the Master did not give you sight when He showered so many other gifts upon you." It sounds hard to believe, but she replied: "Do you know that if at birth I had been able to make one petition, it would have been that I was born blind? . . . Because when I get to heaven, the first face that shall ever gladden my sight will be that of my Savior."

Crosby saw life with an eternal perspective. Our problems look different in light of eternity: "For our light and momentary troubles are achieving for us an eternal glory that far outweighs them all. So we fix our eyes not on what is seen, but on what is unseen, since what is seen is temporary, but what is unseen is eternal" (2 Corinthians 4:17–18).

All our trials dim when we remember that one glorious day we will see Jesus!

—*Dennis Fisher*

"The best we can hope for in this life is a knothole peek at the shining realities ahead. Yet a glimpse is enough." —Joni Eareckson Tada

AN ESCORT THROUGH
THE VALLEY

Read: Psalm 23

Where, O death, is your victory? Where, O death, is your sting?
—1 CORINTHIANS 15:55

I've heard people say, "I'm not afraid of death because I'm confident that I'm going to heaven; it's the dying process that scares me!" Yes, as Christians, we look forward to heaven but may be afraid of dying. We need not be ashamed to admit that. It is natural to be afraid of the pain that comes with dying, of being separated from our loved ones, of possibly impoverishing our families, and of regret over missed earthly opportunities.

Why don't Christians need to be afraid of death itself? Because Jesus was raised from the grave, and we who are in Christ will also be raised. That is why in 1 Corinthians 15:56–57, Paul proclaimed: "The sting of death is sin, and the power of sin is the law. But thanks be to God! He gives us the victory through our Lord Jesus Christ."

The dying process is but an escort that ushers us into eternity with God. As we "walk through the valley of the shadow of death," we can have this confidence from God's Word: "You are with me; Your rod and Your staff, they comfort me" (Psalm 23:4 NKJV). The picture here is of the Lord coming alongside us, giving comfort and direction as He escorts us through the dark valley to the "house of the LORD." There we will dwell with Him forever (v. 6).

—Albert Lee

"Let your hope of heaven master your fear of death." —William Gurnall

ONLY A SKETCH

Read: 1 Corinthians 13:8–12

Now we see only a reflection as in a mirror; then we shall see face to face.
Now I know in part; then I shall know fully, even as I am fully known.
—1 CORINTHIANS 13:12

In *The Weight of Glory*, C. S. Lewis tells the story of a woman who gave birth to a son while confined as a prisoner in a dungeon. Since the boy had never seen the outside world, his mother tried to describe it by making pencil drawings. Later when he and his mother were released from prison, the simple pencil sketches were replaced by the actual images of our beautiful world.

In a similar way, the inspired picture the Bible gives us of heaven will someday be replaced by joyful, direct experience. Paul understood that our perception of heaven is limited until that future day when we will be in Christ's presence. "Now we see only a reflection as in a mirror; then we shall see face to face. Now I know in part; then I shall know fully, even as I am fully known" (1 Corinthians 13:12). Yet Paul's confidence in future glory gave him strength in the midst of trial: "I consider that our present sufferings are not worth comparing with the glory that will be revealed in us" (Romans 8:18).

Our current idea of the glories of heaven is only a simple sketch. But we can be completely confident in Jesus' claim that He has gone to prepare a place for us (John 14:1–3). The best is yet to come!

—*Dennis Fisher*

"Heaven is a realm of unsurpassed joy, unfading glory, undiminished bliss, unlimited delights, and unending pleasures. It will be a perfect existence."
—John MacArthur

ERNIE'S FAREWELL

Read: 2 Corinthians 5:6-8; Philippians 1:21-23

Now is the time of God's favor, now is the day of salvation.
—2 CORINTHIANS 6:2

On September 30, 2009, columnist Mitch Albom sat on stage at the Fox Theater in Detroit, Michigan, to interview Ernie Harwell, one of the most beloved men in American sports. Harwell spent more than fifty years as a radio play-by-play announcer, mostly for the Detroit Tigers baseball team. His kindness, humility, and warmth as a broadcaster left an indelible impression on all who heard him or had the opportunity to meet him.

When Albom interviewed him, Ernie was ninety-one years old and had just announced that he had incurable cancer. But as Ernie talked, he wasn't about to let people feel sorry for him. Instead, he wanted to talk about the night in 1961 when he trusted Jesus Christ as Savior. And, during one of the final times this Hall of Fame announcer would be able to speak publicly, he concluded, "I don't know how many days I've got left . . . [but] I can really know . . . whose arms I'm going to end up in, and what a great, great thing heaven is going to be."

Ernie was anticipating something special! He knew that God had a glorious eternal home prepared for him (John 14:2–3; Philippians 1:21–23), so he could look death in the face and praise God. Is that your confidence? Do you know that His arms are waiting to welcome you home? At the end, that's really all that matters.

—*Dave Branon*

"A continual looking forward to the eternal world is not a form of escapism or wishful thinking, but one of the things a Christian is meant to do." —C. S. Lewis

THE GATHERING

Read: Revelation 7:9-17

The Lamb at the center of the throne will be their shepherd; "he will lead them to springs of living water." —REVELATION 7:17

During Oswald Chambers's service as a YMCA chaplain in Egypt (1915–1917), he touched the lives of many soldiers who would later die in World War I. On November 6, 1916, Chambers wrote in his diary: "We have a letter from a New Zealand friend telling us that Ted Strack has been killed. And so Ted Strack has 'gone to be with Jesus.' That is just how he would have put it. . . . [He] was a rough beauty of nature and of grace, a fearless, loveable little saint. Thank God for every remembrance of him. . . . So they are gathering one by one."

As we grieve the death of those we love, we cling to Jesus's promise of life beyond the grave. The book of Revelation records John's vision of a great multitude from every nation, tribe, and language gathered around God's throne in heaven (7:9). The overarching truth of this passage is a glad, eternal reunion when "The Lamb at the center of the throne will be their shepherd; 'he will lead them to springs of living water' " (v. 17).

The death of all believers in Christ foreshadows the day when we will join them with the Lord. In our sadness today, we are hopeful as we see that "they are gathering one by one."

—*David McCasland*

"The hearts of those in heaven say, 'I want this to go on forever.' And it will. There is no better news than this." –J. I. Packer

"HERE I COME"

Read: Psalm 23

Yea, though I walk through the valley of the shadow of death, I will fear no evil; for You are with me. —PSALM 23:4 (NKJV)

When I was about ten years old, I climbed the big pine tree in our front yard. Grabbing the top branch, I began pulling myself up to get the highest vantage point possible. Suddenly the tip of the old pine snapped, and I came plummeting down! I hit the ground flat on my back. With the wind knocked out of me, I lay gasping for breath. I thought I was dying! I can recall thinking, *I'm going to heaven.* Just before lapsing into unconsciousness, I said with childlike confidence, "Father, here I come."

My dad was studying under a shade tree nearby and heard me come crashing down. Rushing over, he picked me up and carried me into the house. What a surprise when I opened my eyes and found myself on our couch—since I had expected to wake up in heaven. Although my fall was quite upsetting for Mother and Dad, I'm glad I had the experience because it taught me at an early age that Christians can have peace even in the valley of the shadow of death. For believers "to live is Christ and to die is gain" (Philippians 1:21), and "to be absent from the body" is "to be present with the Lord" (2 Corinthians 5:8 NKJV). As children of God, we can live each day with the assurance that whether we live or die, we are the Lord's.

If you know Christ as your Savior, you too can experience a wonderful peace—even if you are called to walk through the "valley of the shadow."

—*Richard DeHaan*

"You will keep in perfect peace those whose minds are steadfast, because they trust in you." —Isaiah 26:3

STAIRWAY TO HEAVEN

Read: John 1:35-51

The Son of Man . . . is the stairway between heaven and earth.
—JOHN 1:51 (NLT)

While traveling in Paris, my husband and I decided to enjoy the view atop the Arch of Triumph. Choosing adventure over ease, we elected to climb the 284 stairs instead of taking the elevator. A good part of the climb was up what seemed like an endless spiral staircase. When we emerged at the apex, we relished the panoramic view of the city—a view made possible by our 162-foot ascent!

In the Old Testament, Jacob dreamed of a stairway that reached from earth to heaven (Genesis 28:12–15). Angels ascended and descended on the structure. And God stood at the top and said, "I am the LORD, the God of your father Abraham" (Genesis 28:13).

Centuries later, Jesus referenced a staircase like the one in Jacob's dream. He had just revealed himself to Nathaniel as the Messiah in a miraculous way (John 1:48–49). To the awestruck new disciple recruit and others, Jesus said, "You will see greater things than this . . . [you'll see] angels of God going up and down on the Son of Man, the one who is the stairway between heaven and earth" (John 1:50–51 NLT).

With this image, Jesus taught the disciples that He was (and is) the way to get to heaven. We can't reach God on our own. He's the One who takes away our sin when we believe in Him.

Those who know Jesus can look forward to spending eternity with Him, our "stairway to heaven."

—Jennifer Benson Schuldt

"To come to Thee is to come home from exile, to come to land out of the raging storm, to come to rest after long labour, to come to the goal of my desires and the summit of my wishes." —Charles Spurgeon

HARD TO IMAGINE

Read: Philippians 1:19-26

*I am torn between the two: I desire to depart and be with Christ,
which is better by far.* —PHILIPPIANS 1:23

Whenever my wife, Martie, and I get ready to go on vacation, we like to read about our destination, study the maps, and anticipate the joy of finally arriving at the place we've dreamed about for so long.

For those of us who know Jesus Christ, we have an incredible destination ahead of us—heaven. But I find it interesting that a lot of us don't seem to be very excited about getting there.

Why is that? Maybe it's because we don't understand heaven. We talk about streets of gold and gates of pearl, but what is it really like? What is there to look forward to?

I think the most profound description of heaven is found in Paul's words to the Philippians. He said that to "depart and be with Christ" is "better by far" (Philippians 1:23). It's what I told my eight-year-old grandson when he asked me what heaven is like. I started by asking him, "What is the most exciting thing in your life?" He told me about his computer game and other fun things he likes to do, and then I told him that heaven is far better. He thought for a minute, and then said, "Papa, that's hard to imagine."

What is it you look forward to in life? What really excites you? Whatever it is, although it's hard to imagine, heaven will be far better!

—*Joe Stowell*

"Earth is receding; heaven is approaching. This is my crowning day."
—Dwight L. Moody

〤

A PLACE TO BE

Read: Nehemiah 1:4-11

My Father's house has many rooms; if that were not so, would I have told you that I am going there to prepare a place for you? —JOHN 14:2

A thousand strands of time, events, and people weave into a tapestry we call *place*. More than just a house, *place* is where meaning, belonging, and safety come together under the covering of our best efforts at unconditional love. *Place* beckons us with memories buried deep in our souls. Even when our *place* isn't perfect, its hold on us is dramatic, magnetic.

The Bible speaks frequently of *place*. We see an example in Nehemiah's longing for a restored Jerusalem (Nehemiah 1:3–4; 2:2). It's no surprise, then, that Jesus would speak of *place* when He wants to comfort us. "Let not your heart be troubled," He began. Then He added: "I go to prepare a *place* for you" (John 14:1–2 NKJV).

For those who have fond memories of earthly places, this promise links us to something we can easily understand and look forward to. And for those whose places have been anything but comforting and safe, Jesus promises that one day they will hear the sweet song that *"place"* sings, for they will inhabit it with Him.

Whatever the struggle, whatever the faltering on your faith journey, remember this: There's a *place* in heaven already waiting, fitted just for you. Jesus wouldn't have said so if it weren't true.

—*Randy Kilgore*

—

We shall not cease from exploration
And at the end of all our exploring
Will be to arrive where we started
And know the place for the first time.
—T. S. Eliot

NEW

Read: 2 Corinthians 5:17-21

I am making everything new! —REVELATION 21:5

Most of us like new things. I'd definitely take a new car to replace my old one. A new fishing boat would be even sweeter. (Oh, how I wish!) Then there are new shoes, new books, new music, new friendships, new opportunities to serve and grow, and more!

New is good. But there's a kind of "new" that the Bible introduces that takes it to a whole new level (no pun intended).

The New Testament uses two different Greek words for the English word *new*. *Neos* refers to something that has recently come into existence, such as a new year. It hadn't existed before and is brand new. *Kainos* speaks of something being *renewed*. It contains the idea that there was something "before" that is now coming into the fullness of its true reality.

The apostle John used *kainos* to describe the future new heaven and new earth (Revelation 21:1). It's the same word he said Jesus will use to proclaim from His throne, "I am making everything new!" (Revelation 21:5). It's also the word the apostle Paul used when he wrote about anyone in Christ becoming a "new creation" (2 Corinthians 5:17). In each case, the idea of "new" is that something that previously existed is being re-created and restored so that it can be all it was meant to be.

Our new creation has already begun! And one day when Christ returns it will be fully revealed.

—*Jeff Olson*

"Something better awaits and beckons us all. We shall be ... full, free, and liberated persons in whom all the possibilities of our God-given humanity will burst forth in undreamed-of fulfillment."
—Bruce Milne, *The Message of Heaven and Hell*

NEW TO THE FAMILY

Read: Luke 15:3-7

There will be more rejoicing in heaven over one sinner who repents than over ninety-nine righteous persons who do not need to repent.
—LUKE 15:7

While on a ministry trip with a Christian high school chorale to Jamaica, we witnessed an illustration of God's love in action. On the day we visited an orphanage for disabled children and teens, we learned that Donald, one of the boys our kids had interacted with, a teen with cerebral palsy, was going to be adopted.

When the adopting couple arrived at the "base" where we were staying, it was a joy to talk to them about Donald. But what was even better was what happened later. We were at the base when Donald and his new parents arrived just after they had picked him up at the orphanage. As the brand-new mom embraced her son, our students gathered around her and sang praise songs. Tears flowed. Tears of joy. And Donald was beaming!

Later, one of the students said to me, "This reminds me of what it must be like in heaven when someone is saved. The angels rejoice because someone has been adopted into God's family." Indeed, it was a picture of the joy of heaven when someone new joins God's forever family by faith in Christ. Jesus spoke of that grand moment when He said, "There will be . . . rejoicing in heaven over one sinner who repents" (Luke 15:7).

Praise God that He has adopted us into His family. No wonder the angels rejoice!

—*Dave Branon*

"Joy is the serious business of heaven." —C. S. Lewis

WE CAN KNOW

Read: 1 John 5:10-15

I write these things to you . . . so that you may know that you have eternal life. —1 JOHN 5:13

As I sat on a train headed for an important appointment, I began to wonder if I was on the right train. I had never traveled that route before and had failed to ask for help. Finally, overcome by uncertainty and doubt, I exited at the next station—only to be told I had indeed been on the right train!

That incident reminded me how doubt can rob us of peace and confidence. At one time I had struggled with the assurance of my salvation, but God helped me deal with my doubt. Later, after sharing the story of my conversion and my assurance that I was going to heaven, someone asked, "How can you be sure you are saved and going to heaven?" I confidently but humbly pointed to the verse that God had used to help me: "I write these things to you who believe in the name of the Son of God so that you may know that you have eternal life" (1 John 5:13).

God promises that through faith in His Son, Jesus, we *already* have eternal life: "God has given us eternal life, and this life is in his Son" (v. 11). This assurance sharpens our faith, lifts us up when we are downhearted, and gives us courage in times of doubt.

—*Lawrence Darmani*

"For I am convinced that neither death nor life, neither angels nor demons, neither the present nor the future, nor any powers, neither height nor depth, nor anything else in all creation, will be able to separate us from the love of God that is in Christ Jesus our Lord." —Paul, Romans 8:38-39

AS IT IS IN HEAVEN

Read: Ephesians 1:9-11

At the right time he will bring everything together under the authority of Christ—everything in heaven and on earth.
—EPHESIANS 1:10 (NLT)

In the Lord's Prayer, Jesus encouraged His followers to pray for God's kingdom to come and His will to be done "on earth as it is in heaven" (Matthew 6:10). Not surprisingly, the four Gospels are loaded with stories of heaven and earth coming together in and around Jesus.

Right from the start, heaven and earth converged in Christ's divine conception. They overlapped when angels appeared to Mary and Joseph to explain her inexplicable pregnancy. It happened again as God sent angels from heaven to announce Jesus' birth.

Heaven and earth continued to join together at Jesus' baptism, when a voice from *heaven* boomed, "You are my Son, whom I love" (Mark 1:11). God's world and our world intersected every time Jesus forgave sins and healed diseases. It happened when the dead were raised to life, when stormy seas were calmed, and when thousands of hungry people were fed with a couple of fish and a few loaves of bread.

For those who have eyes to see, something radically new happened in and through Jesus's coming. He was announcing that people from *all* backgrounds are included and *every* dimension of creation is touched when God's long-awaited kingdom comes "on earth as it is in heaven."

This is what Jesus ignited in His birth and ministry, established through His death and resurrection, and will one day complete when He returns. This is the creation-renewing mission He taught us to pray for and saved us to be a part of today and forever—"on earth as it is in heaven."

—*Jeff Olson*

"This, then, is how you should pray: 'Our Father in heaven, hallowed be your name, your kingdom come, your will be done, on earth as it is in heaven.' "
—Jesus, Matthew 6:9–11

X

THE BEST FISHING HOLES

Read: 2 Corinthians 12:1-4

[He] was caught up to paradise and heard inexpressible things.
—2 CORINTHIANS 12:4

It was a sad day when my friend Gus passed away. Gus was a fellow trout fisherman. Weekends usually found him in his little boat on a nearby lake, casting for fish. I got a letter from his daughter Heidi. She told me she had been talking about heaven with her grandkids since Gus went to his home in heaven. Her six-year-old grandson, who also loves to fish, explained what heaven is like and what Great-Grandpa Gus is doing: "It's really beautiful," he mused, "and Jesus is showing Grandpa Gus where the best fishing holes are."

When Paul reported his God-given vision of heaven, words failed him. He said, "I was caught up to paradise and heard things so astounding that they cannot be expressed in words" (2 Corinthians 12:4 NLT). Words cannot convey the facts of heaven—perhaps because we humans are unable to comprehend them.

While we might gain some comfort from knowing more details about heaven, it is not knowledge about heaven that assures us; it is our knowledge of God himself. Because I know Him and I know how good He is, I can leave this life and everything in it with complete confidence that heaven will be beautiful and Jesus will show me "the best fishing holes"— because that's the kind of God He is!

—*David Roper*

"According to the principal of continuity, we should expect the New Earth to be characterized by familiar, earthly (though uncorrupted) things." —Randy Alcorn, *Heaven*

AND THEN YOU LAUGH

Read: 2 Corinthians 5:1-8

God made him who had no sin to be sin for us, so that in him we might become the righteousness of God. —2 CORINTHIANS 5:21

Noise. Vibration. Pressure. Fireball. Canadian astronaut Chris Hadfield used these words to describe being launched into space. As the rocket raced toward the International Space Station, the weight of gravity increased and breathing became difficult. Just when he thought he would pass out, the rocket made a fiery breakthrough into weightlessness. Instead of lapsing into unconsciousness, he recalls, he broke into laughter.

His description made me think of the days leading to my mother's death. The heaviness of life kept increasing until she no longer had the strength to breathe. She was then released from her pain and could break free into the "weightlessness" of heaven. I like to think of her laughing when she took her first breath in Jesus's presence.

On the Friday we call "Good," something similar happened to Jesus. God placed on Him the weight of the entire world's sin—past, present, and future—until He could no longer breathe. Then He said, "Father, into your hands I commit my spirit" (Luke 23:46). After being suffocated by our sin, Jesus received back from God the life entrusted to Him, and He now lives where sin and death have no power. All who trust Christ will one day join Him, and I wonder if we'll look back at this life and laugh.

—*Julie Ackerman Link*

"The nearer anyone is to heaven, the more earnestly he desires to be there, because Christ is there." —John Owen

MULTIPLY IT

Read: Revelation 22:1-5

No longer will there be any curse. —REVELATION 22:3

Amy had battled cancer for five years. Then the doctor told her that the treatments were failing, and she had just a few weeks to live. Wanting some understanding and assurance about eternity, Amy asked her pastor, "What will heaven be like?"

He asked her what she liked most about her life on earth. She talked about walks and rainbows and caring friends and the laughter of children. "So, then, are you saying I will have all of that there?" she asked longingly.

Amy's pastor replied, "I believe that your life there will be far more beautiful and amazing than anything you ever loved or experienced here. Think about what's best here for you and multiply it over and over and over. That's what I think heaven will be."

The Bible doesn't describe in detail what eternal life will be like, but it does tell us that being with Christ is "better by far" than our present circumstances (Philippians 1:23). "No longer will there be any curse. The throne of God and of the Lamb will be in the city, and his servants will serve him" (Revelation 22:3).

Best of all, we will see the Lord Jesus face to face. Our deepest yearnings will be fully satisfied in Him.

—*Anne Cetas*

"Being with Christ is the very heart of heaven, so we should be confident that we will have unhindered access to him." —Randy Alcorn, *Heaven*

BELONGING

Read: John 14:1-11

*In My Father's house are many mansions; . . . I go to prepare
a place for you.* —JOHN 14:2 (NKJV)

My dad was full of stories about his hometown. So you can
imagine how excited I was as a child when he took our family
there every summer. We fished the St. Joseph River together
and visited his boyhood farm where all his stories came to life.
Although that place was never really my home, whenever I
visit that town—now with grown children and grandchildren
of my own—it fills me with a nostalgic sense of belonging.

Jesus talked with His disciples about His home in heaven,
which He left to come and live among us. What a joy it must
have been for Him to tell His disciples, "In My Father's house
are many mansions; . . . I go to prepare a place for you . . . .
that where I am, there you may be also" (John 14:2–3 NKJV).
No doubt Jesus, who "for the joy set before him . . . endured
the cross" (Hebrews 12:2), was looking forward to returning to
His heavenly home and taking His Father's sons and daughters
there to be with Him.

The thought of Jesus taking us to His Father's home fills us
with great anticipation and compels us to tell others the good
news about the Son.

—*Joe Stowell*

"The way you store up treasure in heaven is by investing in getting
people there." —Rick Warren

ETERNAL EYESIGHT

Read: 2 Corinthians 4:16-5:8

So we fix our eyes not on what is seen, but on what is unseen,
since what is seen is temporary, but what is unseen is eternal.
—2 CORINTHIANS 4:18

I received good news at my eye checkup—my faraway vision had improved. Well, I thought it was good news until a friend informed me: "Faraway vision can improve as we age; close-up vision may diminish."

The report made me think of another kind of improved faraway vision that I have observed in some Christians. Those who have known the Lord for a long time or who have gone through great trials seem to have a better heavenly vision than the rest of us. Their eternal eyesight has gotten better as their close-up "earthly" vision is diminishing.

Because the apostle Paul had that type of eternal vision, he encouraged the church in Corinth: "Our light and momentary troubles are achieving for us an eternal glory that far outweighs them all. So we fix our eyes not on what is seen, but on what is unseen, since what is seen is temporary, but what is unseen is eternal" (2 Corinthians 4:17–18).

For now we struggle with our "eyesight." There's a tension between enjoying all that God has given us in this life, yet still believing what theologian Jonathan Edwards said about our future: "To go to heaven, fully to enjoy God, is infinitely better than the most pleasant accommodations here." Seeing Him will bring perfect vision.

—*Anne Cetas*

"Aim at heaven and you will get earth thrown in. Aim at earth and you get neither." —C. S. Lewis

MYSTERIOUS TRUTH

Read: John 17:20-26

Precious in the sight of the LORD is the death of his faithful servants.
—PSALM 116:15

Sometimes when the infinite God conveys His thoughts to finite man, mystery is the result. For example, there's a profound verse in the book of Psalms that seems to present more questions than answers: "Precious in the sight of the LORD is the death of his faithful servants" (116:15).

I shake my head and wonder how that can be. I have a tough time seeing what is "precious" about the fact that our daughter was taken in a car accident at the age of seventeen—or that any of us have lost cherished loved ones.

We begin to unwrap the mystery, though, when we consider that what is precious to the Lord is not confined to earthly blessings. This verse examines an eternal perspective. For instance, I know from Psalm 139:16 that Melissa's arrival in God's heaven was expected. God was looking for her arrival, and it was precious in His eyes. And think about this: Imagine the Father's joy when He welcomes His children home and sees their absolute ecstasy in being face to face with His Son (see John 17:24).

When death comes for the follower of Christ, God opens His arms to welcome that person into His presence. Even through our tears, we can see how precious that is in God's eyes.

—*Dave Branon*

"Those whom you laid in the grave with many tears are in good keeping: you will see them again with joy. Believe it, think on it, rest on it. It is all true." —J. C. Ryle

WITH THE LORD

Read: 1 Thessalonians 4:13-18

For we believe that Jesus died and rose again, and so we believe that God will bring with Jesus those who have fallen asleep in him.
—1 THESSALONIANS 4:14

Everyone wants to know what heaven will be like, and over the past several years a spate of books have promised to tell them.

These books that claim to provide firsthand accounts of the afterlife have encouraged many, but I'll limit my words to what we find in Scripture. Read Luke 23:43, 2 Corinthians 5:6–8, Philippians 1:21–23, and 1 Thessalonians 4:14, and you'll discover that one thing Scripture says about heaven is that it's where we're with the Lord. This is enough, because the presence of the Lord is what makes heaven "heaven." Why wasn't Lazarus upset when Jesus raised him from the dead? Why didn't he complain? I think he may have been glad to come back to life because Jesus was *there*. Lazarus's house in Bethany had become a corner of heaven.

We get another glimpse of heaven in Revelation 6:9–11. John writes of the martyred saints shouting to the Lord, "How long, Sovereign Lord, holy and true, until you judge the inhabitants of the earth and avenge our blood?" They're not suffering, for they've been delivered from the grasp of sin. But they aren't entirely satisfied either. As great as it is to be a disembodied soul in heaven, there's something even better: to be a whole person living on earth.

And so these saints pray for the return of Jesus and the resurrection of their bodies. Let's join them in John's closing prayer of Scripture, "Amen. Come, Lord Jesus" (Revelation 22:20).

—*Mike Wittmer*

"As Jesus was raised to come back to live on earth, so we will be raised to come back to live on earth." –Randy Alcorn

A PLACE FOR YOU

Read: John 13:36–14:4

Where I am going, you cannot follow now, but you will follow later.
—JOHN 13:36

A couple who brought their elderly aunt to live with them was concerned that she would not feel at home. So they transformed a room in their house into an exact replica of her bedroom at the home she left behind. When their aunt arrived, her furniture, wall hangings, and other favorite things felt like a special "Welcome home!" to her.

In John 13:36–14:4, we read that at the Last Supper Jesus spoke to His disciples and tried to prepare them for His death. When Simon Peter asked, "Where are you going?" Jesus replied, "Where I am going, you cannot follow now, but you will follow later" (13:36). Jesus was still speaking directly to Peter (and also meant it for all of His followers) when He said, "My Father's house has many rooms; if that were not so, would I have told you that I am going there to prepare a place for you? And if I go and prepare a place for you, I will come back and take you to be with me that you also may be where I am" (14:2–3).

Heaven is a family gathering of believers from every tribe and nation, but it is also our Father's house—and in that house He is preparing a room just for you.

When you arrive in heaven and Jesus opens the door, you'll know you're home.

—*David McCasland*

"When Christ calls me home, I shall go with the gladness of a boy bounding away from school." —Adoniram Judson

LESSON IN CRYING

Read: Revelation 21:1-7

Blessed are those who mourn, for they will be comforted.
—MATTHEW 5:4

Has your heart ever been broken? What broke it? Cruelty? Failure? Unfaithfulness? Loss? Perhaps you've crept into the darkness to cry.

It's good to cry. "Tears are the only cure for weeping," said Scottish preacher George MacDonald. A little crying does one good.

Jesus wept at His friend Lazarus's grave (John 11:35), and He weeps with us (v. 33). His heart was broken as well. Our tears attract our Lord's lovingkindness and tender care. He knows our troubled, sleepless nights. His heart aches for us when we mourn. He is the "God of all comfort, who comforts us in all our troubles" (2 Corinthians 1:3–4). And He uses His people to comfort one another.

But tears and our need for comfort come back all too frequently in this life. Present comfort is not the final answer. There is a future day when there will be no death, no sorrow, no crying, for all these things will have "passed away" (Revelation 21:4). God will wipe away every tear. We are so dear to our Father that He will be the one who wipes the tears away from our eyes; He loves us so deeply and so personally.

Remember, "Blessed are those who mourn, for they will be comforted" (Matthew 5:4).

—*David Roper*

"Earth has no sorrow that heaven cannot heal." —Thomas More

A FAMILY REUNION

Read: 1 Thessalonians 2:4-12

We were like young children among you. Just as a nursing mother cares for her children, so we cared for you. —1 THESSALONIANS 2:7–8

For the past several decades, the annual Celebration of Life reunion in our city has brought together members of a unique family. The festive gathering reunites doctors, nurses, and staff from Colorado Springs' Memorial Hospital for Children with former patients from its neonatal intensive care unit. Some are infants in strollers while others are young teens. Their parents have come with them to say thank you to those who saved their children's lives and gave them a second chance. Edward Paik's article in *The Gazette* quoted Dr. Bob Kiley's heartfelt response: "Both professionally and personally, for all the staff, this solidifies why we're in this job."

I wonder if in heaven there will be many such times when spiritual caregivers and the "babes in Christ" they helped will reunite to share stories and give praise to God. The New Testament describes how Paul, Silas, and Timothy worked among the young believers in Thessalonica with gentleness, "just as a nursing mother cares for her children" (1 Thessalonians 2:7), and with comfort and encouragement, "as a father deals with his own children" (v. 11).

Helping new believers at a critical stage in their faith is a labor of love that will be cause for great rejoicing at the "family" reunion in heaven.

—*David McCasland*

"Heaven doesn't make life *less* important;
it makes it *more* important."
—Billy Graham

✕

WE SHALL BE CHANGED

Read: 2 Corinthians 4:16–5:8

We shall be like him, for we shall see him as he is. —1 JOHN 3:2

Being afflicted with early-onset Alzheimer's disease, Thomas DeBaggio chronicled his gradual memory loss in the book *Losing My Mind*. This book records the disturbing process by which—little by little—tasks, places, and people are all forgotten.

Alzheimer's disease involves the failure of nerve cells in the brain, leading to gradual memory loss, confusion, and disorientation. It can be tragic to watch a previously mentally alert person slowly forget how to dress or fail to recognize the faces of loved ones. It's like losing the person before he dies.

Memory loss can occur by other means as well, such as injury or life trauma. And for those of us who live into old age, the breakdown of our bodies is inevitable.

For the Christian, though, there is hope. When believers receive their glorified bodies at the resurrection, they will be perfect (2 Corinthians 5:1–5). But even more important, we will recognize the One who died to redeem us. We will remember what He did and know Him by the nail prints in His hands (John 20:25; 1 Corinthians 13:12).

Forgetfulness may beset our earthly bodies, but when we see the Lord, "We shall be like him, for we shall see him as he is" (1 John 3:2).

—Dennis Fisher

———

"How sweet is rest after fatigue! How sweet will heaven be when our journey is ended." —George Whitefield

RESURRECTION AND LIFE

Read: 1 Corinthians 15:1-11

I am the resurrection and the life. —JOHN 11:25

Jesus said, "I am the resurrection and the life." It's one thing to make such a bold assertion; it's another to back it up—and back it up Jesus did by rising from the dead.

"If you believe that the Son of God died and rose again," writes George MacDonald, "your whole future is full of the dawn of eternal morning, coming up beyond the hills of life, and full of such hope as the highest imagination for the poet has not a glimmer yet."

The Son of God died and rose again, and His resurrection is the guarantee that God will bring us up and out of the ground: A thinking, feeling, remembering, recognizable person will live forever.

Living forever means living out the thought of eternity that God has placed in our hearts; meeting again one's believing loved ones lost through separating death; living in a world without sorrow; seeing our Lord who loves us and gave everything to unite us to Him forever.

But I see another meaning. Since we have this life and the next, we don't need to "have it all" now. We can live in broken and ruined bodies for a time; we can endure poverty and hardship for a while; we can face loneliness, heartache, and pain for a season. Why? There is a second birth—eternal life with God.

—David Roper

"Christians have a dual citizenship—on earth and in heaven—and our citizenship in heaven ought to make us better people here on earth." —Warren Wiersbe, *Be Joyful*

MUST-SEE DESTINATIONS

Read: Romans 8:19-25

Creation itself will be liberated from its bondage to decay and brought into the freedom and glory of the children of God. —ROMANS 8:21

The title of a 2010 *LIFE* special edition magazine reads: "Heaven on Earth: The World's Must-See Destinations." It contains stunning photography of places such as the Grand Canyon, Alaska's Denali, Petra in Jordan, and Rio de Janeiro. I've been fortunate enough to visit a few of them.

This magazine caught my attention shortly after the death of my parents. Both my mom and dad went to be with Jesus in 2012. In the months following their deaths, I found myself grieving over the "must-see destinations" my folks were never able to visit.

The hope, however, of a renewed earth brings me great comfort. The world currently groans under the crushing weight of sin and decay (Romans 8:21–22). But when God comes back to dwell with us forever, He will fully and completely bring heaven to earth. All the broken effects of sin will be gone forever and Jesus will renew all things (Revelation 21:1–5), including the physical earth—reclaiming its original goodness (Genesis 1:31).

The profound implications of a renewed earth are too many to name here, but in the midst of grief I find comfort in knowing that my parents (along with all of God's forgiven and restored children) will have the rest of eternity to visit all of the "must-see destinations" the new heaven and earth will offer.

—*Jeff Olson*

"Throughout eternity we will live full, truly human lives, exploring and managing God's creation to his glory. Fascinating vistas will unfold before us as we learn to serve God in a renewed universe." —Edward Donnelly, *Biblical Teaching on the Doctrines of Heaven and Hell*

FEARFUL TEARS

Read: Revelation 5:1–12

I wept and wept because no one was found who was worthy to open the scroll or look inside. —REVELATION 5:4

John, the great apostle and the one Jesus loved, was reduced to tears.

In a vision he received while imprisoned (Revelation 5:1–12), he found himself in God's throne room as future events unfolded. In heaven, John saw God hold up a sealed scroll. He wept because as he observed the glories of God's presence, he saw no one who could open the scroll—no one with the power to reveal God's final revelation and to complete the concluding chapter of history's drama.

As an apostle, John had observed the power of sin in the world. He had witnessed Jesus's life and death on earth to conquer sin. He had seen Him ascend into heaven. But now he was fearful when he saw that no one was worthy to open the scroll and vanquish sin forever (v. 4).

Imagine the drama of what happened next. An elder approached John and said, "Do not weep!" And he pointed him toward Someone he knew: "See, the Lion of the tribe of Judah" (v. 5). John looked, and he saw Jesus—the only One with the power to take the scroll, open the seals, and complete the story. Soon John's tears were dry, and millions of angels were proclaiming, "Worthy is the Lamb" (v. 12).

Are you crying? Behold John's friend—Jesus. He is worthy. Turn things over to Him.

—*Dave Branon*

"Take the world but give me Jesus." —Fanny Crosby

ANTICIPATION

Read: 1 Thessalonians 4:13-18

*I will come back and take you to be with me that you also
may be where I am.* —JOHN 14:3

At the beginning of each March, my friend begins a count-down. Marked on the calendar in her office are the twenty days left until the first day of spring. One morning when I saw her, she volunteered, "Only twelve more days!" A few days later, "Only six!" Her enthusiasm started to rub off on me, and I began to keep track as well. "Just two more days, Jerrie!" "I know!" she beamed.

As believers, we have something to look forward to that is even more exciting than the anticipation of budding flowers and lots of sunshine after a long winter. God has made many promises in His Word, and each one has been or will be ful-filled. But the certainty that Christ will return is one of the greatest promises of all. "For the Lord himself will come down from heaven, with a loud command, with the voice of an arch-angel and with the trumpet call of God . . . . After that, we who are still alive and are left will be caught up together with them in the clouds to meet the Lord in the air. And so we will be with the Lord forever" (1 Thessalonians 4:16–17).

Although no one can know the exact day, we have God's promise that Jesus will come back (Acts 1:7–11). Each year when we celebrate spring and the coming Easter season, let's encourage each other in anticipation of that day!

—*Cindy Hess Kasper*

"Nothing is more prominently brought forward in the New Testament than the second coming of the Lord Jesus Christ." —John Nelson Darby

✕

PERFECT PEACE AND REST

Read: Psalm 71:19-24

Though you have made me see troubles, many and bitter,
you will restore my life again. —PSALM 71:20

The psalmist had seen "troubles, many and bitter" (Psalm 71:20). Yet hovering in the back of his mind was the thought that God would "restore" him again. The literal meaning of this phrase is "bring him to life again." He elaborated: "From the depths of the earth [the grave] you will again bring me up. You will increase my honor and comfort me once more" (vv. 20–21). If the troubles didn't end in this life, certainly in heaven they would.

This thought—that someday we shall be in God's presence and enjoy Him forever—crowns many of the psalms and is an assurance that helps life's present troubles fade away (see Psalms 16, 17, 49, 73).

Perhaps no one but God knows the trouble you've seen, but this life is not all that will be. Someday, your Father will "increase [your] greatness"—you will be clothed with unspeakable glory. And there will be comfort "on every side" (Psalm 71:21 NKJV). His presence and love will bring perfect peace and rest.

Seventeenth-century clergyman Richard Baxter wrote, "O what a blessed day that will be when I shall . . . stand on the shore and look back on the raging seas I have safely passed; when I shall review my pains and sorrows, my fears and tears, and possess the glory which was the end of all!"

—*David Roper*

"I may not long for death, but I surely long for heaven." –Joseph Bayly, *A Voice in the Wilderness*

IMAGINE

Read: John 14:1-6

Do not let not your hearts be troubled. —JOHN 14:1

Our church's young people did what they could to "construct heaven." It was time for the spring banquet, and the creative teens used lights, Styrofoam, and other materials to turn the auditorium into their best idea of heaven.

The theme of the banquet was "I Can Only Imagine," from the song by MercyMe. Our high school junior daughter Melissa helped transform the church. When I visited to see how the kids were doing, she was in the rafters hanging stars. The night of the banquet, my wife and I were able to hear one of Melissa's friends sing the theme song as we all thought about this faraway place called heaven.

Of course, we never could have imagined that Melissa would be entering the real heaven just six weeks later after a car accident. The imaginary would become reality.

Jesus told us about heaven as a way of untroubling our hearts. He said, "Do not let not your hearts be troubled. . . . My Father's house has many rooms; if that were not so, would I have told you that I am going there to prepare a place for you?" (John 14:1–2).

Heaven is a prepared place for prepared hearts—a place of unimaginable beauty, splendor, and majesty. It's where God is caring for our believing loved ones, and someday for us. Imagine heaven, and rejoice!

—Dave Branon

"I pity the man who never thinks about heaven." —J. C. Ryle

BEYOND IMAGINATION

Read: Revelation 21:1–8

No human mind has conceived—the things God has prepared for those who love him. —1 CORINTHIANS 2:9

A college professor at a Christian school perceived that his students held a distorted view of heaven; they considered it to be static and boring. So, to stir their imaginations, he asked them these questions:

"Do you wish you would wake up tomorrow morning to discover that the person you loved most passionately loved you even more? Wake up hearing music you have always loved but had never heard with such infinite joy before? Rise to the new day as if you were just discovering the Pacific Ocean? Wake up without feeling guilty about anything at all? See to the very core of yourself, and like everything you see? Wake up breathing God as if He were air? Loving to love Him? And loving everybody else in the bargain?"

In response to that professor's intriguing questions, the students all lifted their hands. If that's what heaven will be like, and even infinitely more so, they certainly wanted to be there.

We all share the desire—really a deep-down yearning—to be in that glorious home forever. It is a place of indescribable bliss. And the supreme blessing will be the presence of our Lord Jesus Christ himself!

—Vernon Grounds

"It's not the jasper walls and the pearly gates that are going to make heaven attractive. It is the being with God." –Dwight Moody

FIVE PEOPLE YOU MEET IN HEAVEN

Read: 2 Corinthians 5:6-11

We must all appear before the judgment seat of Christ.
—2 CORINTHIANS 5:10

Mitch Albom, author of *The Five People You Meet in Heaven,* said that he got the idea for his book when he speculated: What would heaven be like if it were a place where some of the people you affected on earth explained your life when you met them in heaven?

Albom's book does give insight into how we unintentionally affect others' lives. But for the Christian, our ultimate joy in eternity does not stem from other people but from our Lord and Savior. Heaven is a real place that Jesus is now preparing for us. And when we get there, we'll rejoice to meet the living Christ (John 14:2–3; 2 Peter 3:13).

This encounter with Jesus, however, will also include accountability for the life we lived on earth. Believers are told: "We must all appear before the judgment seat of Christ, so that each of us may receive what is due us for the things done while in the body, whether good or bad" (2 Corinthians 5:10). His wise and just evaluation will show us how well we have loved God and our neighbor (Matthew 22:37–40).

We don't know who will be the first five people we meet in heaven. But we do know who the most important One will be—the Lord Jesus.

—*Dennis Fisher*

"The most exhilarating experiences on earth . . . will seem tame to the thrill of seeing Jesus." —Randy Alcorn, *Heaven*

PRELUDE OF PRAISE

Read: Psalm 150

I will ever sing in praise of your name and fulfill my vows day after day.
—PSALM 61:8

We enter a concert hall, find our seats, and listen with anticipation as the members of the orchestra tune their instruments. The sound is discordant, not melodic. But the tuning is simply a prelude to the symphony.

C. S. Lewis suggested that's how it is with our devotional practices and even our worship services. Sometimes they sound discordant, but God hears our prayers and praises with fatherly delight. We are really preparing for participation in the glorious symphony of heaven. Now we are making a minuscule contribution to the harmonies of angelic and redeemed hosts. But our adoration, though feeble, pleases the heart of the Divine Listener more than the finest rendition of earth's greatest orchestra.

Are we eagerly awaiting our participation in heaven's symphony of praise? Are we joyfully participating in the adoration that delights the heart of God? Or do we regard devotion as more of a discipline than a delight?

Our attitudes will be transformed when we realize that praise delights God's heart. Praise helps us to tune our lives to heavenly harmonies.

Praise is an indispensable preparation for the worship that will be our eternal joy. "Let everything that has breath praise the LORD" (Psalm 150:6).

—*Vernon Grounds*

"Enter his gates with thanksgiving,
and his courts with praise."

—the psalmist, Psalm 100:4

GOOD TO BE HOME

Read: Psalm 73:21-28

You guide me with your counsel, and afterward you will take me into glory.
—PSALM 73:24

One of my favorite pastimes as a boy was walking the creek behind our home. Those walks were high adventure for me: rocks to skip, birds to watch, dams to build, animal tracks to follow. And if I made it to the mouth of the creek, my dog and I would sit and share lunch while we watched the biplanes land across the lake.

We'd linger as long as we could, but only so long, for my father wanted me home before sunset. The shadows grew long and the hollows got dark fast in the woods. I'd be wishing along the way that I was already home.

Our house sat on a hill behind some trees, but the light was always on until all the family was in. Often my father would be sitting on the back porch, reading the paper, waiting for me. "How did it go?" he would ask. "Pretty good," I'd say. "But it sure is good to be home."

Those memories of walking that creek make me think of another journey—the one I'm making now. It isn't always easy, but I know at the end of it there's a caring Father and my eternal home. I can hardly wait to get there.

I'm expected there. The light is on and my heavenly Father is waiting for me. I suppose He'll ask, just like my father used to, "How did it go?" "Pretty good," I'll say. "But it sure is good to be Home."

—David Roper

"Our deepest instinct is heaven. Heaven is the ache in our bones, the splinter in our heart." —Mark Buchanan, *Things Unseen*

A HAPPY REUNION

Read: Revelation 21:1-5

Look! God's dwelling place is now among the people, and he will dwell with them. They will be his people, and God himself will be with them and be their God. —REVELATION 21:3

In 2002, Elizabeth Smart was kidnapped from her home in Utah. She lived a vagabond life in the constant presence of the couple who abducted her. However, nine months after she was kidnapped she was found and returned home. It was the happy reunion her family had been longing for.

In the book of Revelation, John describes a vision of a new heaven and a new earth and our future reunion with the Lord (21:1–5). The context is not just geographic but a context of life for God's people—a glorious reality of God and His people dwelling together for eternity.

John describes the benefits that come to God's people when He takes up His abode in their midst. Abolished forever are the debilitating consequences of sin. In John's vision, sorrow, death, pain, and separation are all part of the first things that are now gone. The old order gives way to the new and perfect order—a reunion of eternal blessedness. "Look! God's dwelling place is now among the people, and he will dwell with them. They will be his people . . . . He who was seated on the throne said, 'I am making everything new!' " (Revelation 21:3, 5).

One day, we'll rejoice over a happy reunion with our heavenly Father. We cannot imagine what a day of rejoicing that will be!

—*Marvin Williams*

"God destines us for an end beyond the grasp of reason."
—Thomas Aquinas

WAITING FOR JOY

Read: 2 Corinthians 4:8-18

Weeping may stay for the night, but rejoicing comes in the morning.
—PSALM 30:5

A large part of life centers on anticipation. How much we would lose if we were to wake up one day to the unexpected announcement: "Christmas in ten minutes!" The enjoyment in many of life's events is built on the fact that we have time to anticipate them.

Christmas, vacations, mission trips, sporting events. All grow in value because of the hours we spend looking forward to them—eagerly running through our minds the fun, challenges, and excitement they'll bring.

I think about the value of anticipation and the thrill it can bring to the human heart when I read Psalm 30:5, "Weeping may stay for the night, but rejoicing comes in the morning." The psalmist is declaring the comforting idea that our sorrow lasts but a short time when compared with the anticipated joy that will begin in heaven and last forever. Paul pens a similar idea in 2 Corinthians 4:17, where we discover that our "light and momentary troubles" lead to a glory of eternal value.

For now, those of us who weep can dwell on hope instead of hopelessness and anticipation instead of sorrow. It may be nighttime in our hearts, but just ahead lies the dawn of eternity. And with it, God promises the endless joy of heavenly morning.

—*Dave Branon*

"The most thrilling thing about heaven is that Jesus Christ will be there. I will see Him face to face. Jesus Christ will meet us at the end of life's journey." —Billy Graham

THE PERSON MAKES
THE PLACE

Read: Revelation 22:6-17

God himself will be with them and be their God. He will wipe every tear from their eyes. —REVELATION 21:3–4

Engaged couples often spend hours poring over travel brochures and vacation websites looking for just the right honeymoon spot. They can hardly wait for their romantic getaway. But it's not so much about the place; it's about being with the person they love.

We get used to places no matter how glorious they are. But being with a person who loves us never gets old!

In Revelation, John paints a beautiful picture of what the new earth will be like. But it's not really about the place—it's about the Person we'll be with. The day is coming when Jesus will return. And the wonderful news is that He says: "Look, I am coming soon!" (22:7).

If you're thinking, *He may come for others, but surely not for me,* don't miss verse 17: "The Spirit and the bride say, 'Come!' And let the one who hears say, 'Come!' Let the one who is thirsty come; and let the one who wishes take the free gift of the water of life." Anyone is welcome to join the wedding feast. All we have to do is believe in the One who died for us, Jesus Christ, the Lover of our souls.

Make no mistake; the new heavens and new earth will be incredible beyond our dreams. But our greatest joy will be the experience of being with Jesus forever!

—*Joe Stowell*

"In nature, everything moves in the direction of its hungers. In the spiritual world it is not otherwise. We gravitate toward our inward longing, provided of course that those longings are strong enough to move us." —A. W. Tozer

CHANGED LANDSCAPE

Read: Matthew 4:1-11

Jesus was led by the Spirit into the wilderness to be tempted by the devil.
—MATTHEW 4:1

I love my garden. But winters in the US Midwest reduce my beautiful garden to a frozen, snow-covered, barren landscape.

It wasn't like that in Eden. Eden was a breathtakingly beautiful garden year-round. And it was in this garden that Adam and Eve basked in the stunning creation of God and the joy of perfect harmony with Him and with each other. Until, that is, Satan arrived on the scene, bringing weeds, thorns, destruction, and death.

You can't help but notice the contrast between the landscape in Genesis 1 and Matthew 4. The same tempter who once entered God's garden now welcomes God to his turf—the dangerous, barren wilderness.

The wilderness can be a picture of what the world—and life—becomes when Satan has his way. With one decisive blow, the joy of Eden was replaced with the barrenness of shame (Genesis 3). But Jesus was victorious on Satan's turf! (Matthew 4). In that victory He gives us hope that we too can have victory—a victory that shows us the enemy no longer holds sway. And a victory that assures us the day is coming when Jesus will return and restore the joy of Eden forever.

Now that's something to look forward to!

—*Joe Stowell*

"The best things in life are souvenirs from Eden, appetizers of the New Earth. There are just enough of them to keep us going but never enough to make us satisfied with the world as it is or ourselves as we are. We live between Eden and New Earth, pulled toward what we once were and what we yet will be."
—Randy Alcorn, *We Shall See God*

※

THE HEAVEN FILE

Read: 1 Thessalonians 4:13-18

We who are still alive and are left will be caught up together with them in the clouds to meet the Lord in the air. —1 THESSALONIANS 4:17

My wife, Luann, has a folder she calls her "heaven file." It contains articles, obituaries, and photos, along with cards from the memorial services of family and friends. She keeps them, not as a sad reminder of people we have loved and lost, but in anticipation of our glad reunion with them in heaven.

Paul wrote of this wonderful expectation to the Christians in Thessalonica, so they would not grieve like people who have no hope. "For the Lord himself will come down from heaven, with a loud command, . . . and the dead in Christ will rise first. After that, we who are still alive and are left will be caught up together with them in the clouds to meet the Lord in the air. And so we will be with the Lord forever. Therefore encourage one another with these words" (1 Thessalonians 4:16–18).

This passage speaks of our future joy together in the presence of Jesus Christ our Savior. For now, we have fellowship with the Lord, and we experience what hymn writer Samuel J. Stone called "mystic sweet communion with those whose rest is won."

Much about the future remains a mystery, but we can confidently look forward to being in the presence of Christ with all the saints who have gone ahead.

—*David McCasland*

"We eagerly await a Savior from [heaven], the Lord Jesus Christ."
—Apostle Paul, Philippians 3:20

OUR DWELLING PLACE

Read: Genesis 12:1-8

By faith Abraham . . . obeyed and went, even though he did not know where he was going. —HEBREWS 11:8

When Abraham was seventy-five years old, God called him to leave the land of his father. And so, advanced in years, he departed for the land of Canaan. He was rootless, homeless, "did not know where he was going" (Hebrews 11:8). That was the story of Abraham's life.

Age brings change and uncertainty. It means transition from a familiar past to an uncertain future. It can mean movement from a family home to a smaller place, to a daughter's home, to a retirement village, to a nursing home—the "final resort." Like Abraham, some of us make our way from one location to another, always traveling and not knowing where we're going.

Yet we can be at home in any dwelling, for our safekeeping lies not in the place where we live but in God himself. We can dwell "in the shelter of the Most High" and "rest in the shadow of the Almighty" (Psalm 91:1). There, in His presence, under His wings, we find refuge (v. 4). The eternal God becomes our dwelling place (v. 9).

Although our dwelling place here on earth may be uncertain, God will be our companion and friend until our traveling days are over and we reach our heart's true home. Until that day, let's shed the light of God's lovingkindness on other travelers.

—David Roper

"The fact that our heart yearns for something earth can't supply is proof that heaven must be our home." —C. S. Lewis

CHANGE OF ADDRESS

Read: 2 Corinthians 5:1-10

I am torn between the two: I desire to depart and be with Christ, which is better by far. —PHILIPPIANS 1:23

Every twenty-six years or so, we move to a different house.

Actually, Sue and I moved into our first home when our first child was a baby. We had no idea we would live there for twenty-six years. When we finally did change our residence, it was an emotional time.

On the day we moved, after everything was out of the house, we did one final walk-through to relive the memories. The toughest moment came when we entered teenager Melissa's bedroom. We had said goodbye to her two years earlier after a car accident took her earthly life. Now we were bidding adieu to the sunflower-decorated room she loved so much.

As I think of that emotional time when we moved, I am reminded of what a great change of address Melissa enjoyed on the day she was ushered into God's presence. Our move to a different house pales in comparison to the glories our daughter now enjoys in heaven. What a grand comfort to know that our departed loved ones who have trusted in Jesus are now living in God's majestic kingdom! (2 Corinthians 5:1).

Are you ready for that ultimate change of address? No matter where you live on this earth, make sure your final home will be heaven.

—*Dave Branon*

"Heaven is not here, it's there. If we were given all we wanted here, our hearts would settle for this world rather than the next." —Elisabeth Elliot

"THERE'S HEAVEN"

Read: Luke 10:19-21

"Rejoice that your names are written in heaven." —LUKE 10:20

When three-year-old Bree's grandpa suffered heart failure, he was taken to a local hospital where he was pronounced dead. A few weeks after the funeral when Bree and her family drove past the hospital, she pointed to it and remarked matter-of-factly, "There's heaven." She knew her grandpa was in heaven. Since he went to the hospital on the day he died, she thought it must be heaven.

Bree's mother wrote, "We adults [have] abstract concepts of a paradise beyond even the invisible stars." Bree's childish view of heaven caused her mom to think of heaven as a real place—which helped to comfort her.

Words are inadequate to describe heaven, but we know it's a real place for those who have trusted Jesus as their Savior. Jesus assures us, "My Father's house has many rooms; if that were not so, would I have told you that I am going to prepare a place for you?" (John 14:2). One day we'll be there, and we won't need to simply imagine it anymore.

—*Anne Cetas*

"There is no man that goes to heaven but he must go by the cross."
—James H. Aughey

SURRENDERED CROWNS

Read: Revelation 4:6-11

You are worthy, our Lord and God, to receive glory and honor and power.
—REVELATION 4:11

Once during her reign, Britain's Queen Victoria (she ruled from 1837 until 1901) listened to a chaplain preach a sermon about the second coming of Christ. Those near the royal box noticed that the queen's eyes were filled with tears.

When the service ended, she asked to see the chaplain alone. Seeing her great emotion, he asked why she was so moved. She replied, "Because of what you said about the coming again of the world's rightful King, I wish still to be here when He returns that I might lay my crown at His blessed feet!"

There are many incentives for faithful service that involve both our acts and our motives. These rewards, which are designated as "crowns" in the New Testament, are to be earned by those who have first received the gift of eternal life.

Perhaps you're saying, "I would never expect to be rewarded for what I do for Christ." Have you considered what you may do with any crown you receive on that day? There will be no trophy cases in heaven; no gloating over earthly accomplishments. Redeemed sinners will have the transcendent joy of casting their crowns before the throne and saying, "You are worthy, our Lord and God, to receive glory and honor and power" (Revelation 4:11).

—*Paul Van Gorder*

"There are no crown-wearers in heaven who were not cross-bearers here below."
—Charles Spurgeon

☩

TEARS IN HEAVEN

Read: Revelation 21:1-8

[God] will wipe every tear from their eyes. There will be no more
death or mourning or crying. —REVELATION 21:4

In 1991, famed British guitarist Eric Clapton was stricken with grief when his four-year-old son Conor died as a result of a fall from an apartment window. Looking for an outlet for his grief, Clapton penned perhaps his most poignant ballad: "Tears in Heaven." It seems that every note weighs heavy with the sense of pain and loss that can be understood only by a parent who has lost a child.

Surprisingly, however, Clapton said in a television interview years later, "In a sense, it wasn't even a sad song. It was a song of belief. When it [says that] there will be no more tears in heaven, I think it's a song of optimism—of reunion."

The thought of a heavenly reunion is powerful indeed. For everyone who has trusted Jesus Christ for salvation, there is the hope that we will be reunited forever in a place where "[God] will wipe every tear from [our] eyes. There will be no more death or mourning or crying" (Revelation 21:4). And, most of all, it is a place where we will "see his face" and forever be with Christ himself (22:4).

In our times of loss and grief, of tears and sorrow, isn't it comforting to know that Christ has purchased for us a home where there will be no more tears!

—Bill Crowder

"When we see death, we see disaster. When Jesus sees death, he sees deliverance." —Max Lucado, *He Still Moves Stones*

THE FAR SIDE OF THE WORLD

Read: Colossians 3:1-4

Our citizenship is in heaven. —PHILIPPIANS 3:20

Patrick O'Brian (1914–2000) is a celebrated author of historical novels. In 1969 he published *Master and Commander*, a novel (later turned into a successful movie with the subtitle *The Far Side of the World*) about naval warfare during the Napoleonic War. One reason for this book's popularity is O'Brian's careful attention to navy lore and natural history with penetrating insights into human nature.

In one stirring scene, Captain Jack Aubrey prepares his crew for battle. He tells them: "England is under threat of invasion, and though we be on the far side of the world, this ship is our home. This ship is England."

Captain Aubrey's view of citizenship is based on loyalty, not location. And this conviction illustrates a biblical principle. Paul wrote to the church at Philippi, a Roman colony: "Our citizenship is in heaven. And we eagerly await a Savior from there, the Lord Jesus Christ" (Philippians 3:20).

It is important for us to be reminded that though we are living on this side of heaven for now, our eternal home is the place where our loyalty should lie. We need to "set [our] minds on things above, not on earthly things" (Colossians 3:2).

—*Dennis Fisher*

"If our treasure is in heaven, we do not need to persuade ourselves that it is; we prove it is by the way we deal with matters of earth." —Oswald Chambers

PRACTICING RESURRECTION

Read: 1 Corinthians 15:20-58

My dear brothers and sisters, stand firm. Let nothing move you. Always give yourselves fully to the work of the Lord, because you know that your labor in the Lord is not in vain. —1 CORINTHIANS 15:58

Believers in Jesus look forward to two great events in the future: our resurrected bodies and the "resurrection" of our groaning planet into a new heaven and earth full of beauty, healing, justice, and joy (Revelation 21:1–23).

But while these are future events, they're to guide our lives *today.* Jesus calls us to pray God's will be done on earth, not just "in heaven" (Matthew 6:10). Paul ends his lengthy explanation of resurrection with a call to action: We're to "give [ourselves] fully to the work of the Lord" (1 Corinthians 15:58). So how can our future hope shape our present work?

We can take inspiration from groups such as The Simple Way community. Years ago Shane Claiborne and some friends moved into a city district where poverty and crime are plentiful. There they've "practiced resurrection" by painting murals on the walls of old tenement blocks and turning abandoned buildings into community centers. When a child mentioned that it was "easier to get a gun in our neighborhood than to get a salad," The Simple Way community built a greenhouse to grow vegetables to share. The community has gone about making ugly things beautiful and bringing dead things to life.

Following Jesus, Shane and his friends are giving their city a glimpse of what resurrection life looks like. They're displaying that "[our] labor in the Lord is not in vain" (1 Corinthians 15:58).

—Sheridan Voysey

"The attributes of God are to be seen in the visible creation, but they are to be seen in a brighter and superior light in the new creation." —Charles Spurgeon

"I'LL PAY YOU LATER"

Read: Luke 14:7-14

You will be repaid at the resurrection of the righteous. —LUKE 14:14

Suppose a boss were to say to an employee, "We really appreciate what you're doing around here, but we've decided to change the way we pay you. Starting today, we're going to pay you later—after you retire." Would the employee jump for joy? Of course not. That's not the way things work in this world. We like our payment now—or at least every payday.

Did you know that God promises to "pay" us later—much later? And He asks us to be happy about it!

Jesus suggested that our ultimate reward for the good things we do in His name comes after we die. In Luke 14, Jesus said that if we care for the poor, the lame, and the blind, our reward for such kindness will come at the resurrection of the righteous (Luke 14:14). He also said that if we are persecuted, we should "rejoice in that day and leap for joy, because great is [our] reward in heaven" (6:23). Surely, the Lord gives us comfort, love, and guidance today, but what additional wonderful things He has planned for us in the future!

This may not be the way we would have planned it; we don't enjoy waiting for things. But imagine how glorious it will be when we receive our rewards in Jesus's presence! What a grand time we'll have as we enjoy what God has reserved for later.

—*Dave Branon*

"A scroll of remembrance was written in his presence concerning those who feared the LORD and honored his name. 'On the day when I act,' says the LORD Almighty, 'they will be my treasured possession. . . . And you will again see the distinction between the righteous and the wicked, between those who serve God and those who do not." —Malachi 3:16-18

EAGER FOR HEAVEN

Read: Philippians 1:19-26

The great street of the city was of gold, as pure as transparent glass.
—REVELATION 21:21

My neighbor Jasmine, age nine, was sitting on the front porch with one summer evening. Out of the blue she started talking about her bad choices and how she needed God's forgiveness. We talked and prayed together, and she asked Jesus to be her Savior.

Questions about heaven started pouring out of her: "Are the streets really gold? Will my mom be there? What if she isn't? Will I have a bed, or will I sleep on a cloud? What will I eat?" I assured her that heaven would be a perfect home, and that she would be with Jesus, who would give her everything she needed. She replied with excitement, "Well, then, let's go right now!"

The apostle Paul had a heavenly perspective too (Philippians 1:23). His testimony was, "To me, to live is Christ and to die is gain" (v. 21). He knew that this life was about knowing, trusting, and serving God. But he also knew that life in heaven would be "better by far" because he would "be with Christ" (v. 23). He wanted to stay here so he could minister to the Philippians and others, but he was ready to go to heaven at any time to see Jesus.

Jasmine is ready to go now. Are we as eager for heaven as she is?

—Anne Cetas

"For the Christian, death is not the end of adventure but a doorway from a world where dreams and adventures shrink, to a world where dreams and adventures forever expand." —Randy Alcorn, *Heaven*

꘎

AMAZING LOVE

Read: John 6:32-40

*For I have come down from heaven not to do my will but to do
the will of him who sent me.* —JOHN 6:38

Approaching the first Christmas after her husband died, our
friend Davidene wrote a remarkable letter in which she pic-
tured what it might have been like in heaven when Jesus was
born on earth. "It was what God always knew would happen,"
she wrote. "The three were one, and He had agreed to allow
the fracturing of His precious unity for our sake. Heaven was
left empty of God the Son."

As Jesus taught and healed people on earth, He said, "I have
come down from heaven not to do my will but to do the will of
him who sent me. . . . For my Father's will is that everyone who
looks to the Son and believes in him shall have eternal life, and
I will raise them up at the last day" (John 6:38, 40).

When Jesus was born in Bethlehem, it was the beginning of
His mission on earth to demonstrate God's love and give His
life on the cross to free us from the penalty and power of sin.

"I cannot imagine actually choosing to let go of the one
I loved, with whom I was one, for the sake of anyone else,"
Davidene concluded. "But God did. He faced a house much
emptier than mine, so that I could live in His house with Him
forever."

"For God so loved the world that he gave his one and only
Son" (John 3:16).

—David McCasland

**"Jesus's coming to earth was a voluntary act of amazing grace, the
almighty Sovereign stooping to become earth's lowly Servant."
—Lehman Strauss**

"HE'S IN HEAVEN"

Read: 2 Corinthians 5:1-8

For to me, to live is Christ and to die is gain. —PHILIPPIANS 1:21

On August 28, 2003, my good friend Kurt DeHaan, at the time the managing editor of *Our Daily Bread,* died of a heart attack while on his lunchtime run. When I learned the news, I said to myself, "He's in heaven," which brought me great comfort.

A few days later I was talking with my former pastor Roy Williamson, then in his eighties. I asked him about a man from our congregation. "He's in heaven," he said. I also inquired about another person. "She's in heaven too," he replied. Then, eyes twinkling, he said, "I know more people in heaven than I do on earth."

Later I was thinking about Pastor Williamson's words. He could have simply said, "He died," or "She died." But how reassuring to hear that those dear saints of God are in heaven. What joy to know that when believers in Christ die, they are instantly with Jesus! The apostle Paul put it like this: "We are confident, I say, and would prefer to be away from the body and at home with the Lord" (2 Corinthians 5:8). No more pain. No more sadness. No more sin. Only peace. Only joy. Only glory.

We still grieve when a believing loved one dies. Grief is love's expression. But beneath it all is an unshakable joy, because we know our loved one is in heaven.

—David Egner

"I suspect that every saved soul in heaven is a great wonder, and that heaven is a vast museum of wonders of grace and mercy—a palace of miracles, in which everything will surprise everyone who gets there." —Charles Spurgeon

A NEW SONG

Read: Psalm 33:1-5

Praise the LORD with the harp; make music to him on the ten-stringed lyre.
Sing to him a new song. —PSALM 33:2–3

I was walking in the park one morning, listening to a tape by the Brooklyn Tabernacle Choir. I had my ancient Walkman clipped to my belt and my headphones clamped over my ears, tuned in to another world. The music was joyous! Oblivious to my surroundings, I began to sing and dance.

Then I spied my neighbor, leaning against a tree with a bemused look on her face. She couldn't hear my music, but she was delighted by my behavior. I wish she could have heard my song.

I thought afterward of the new song God has placed in our hearts, a song we hear from another world. It tells us that God loves us and always will, that He has "rescued us from the dominion of darkness" (Colossians 1:13), and that He has "seated us with him in the heavenly realms in Christ Jesus" (Ephesians 2:6). And someday we'll be with Him forever.

In the meantime He has given us eternally useful things to do. Grace now and glory ahead! Is this not a reason to sing?

Next time you're feeling down, think about God's goodness. Tune in to the music of heaven and sing a new song with the angels. It may set your feet to dancing and cause great wonderment in those around you. Perhaps they'll want to hear the music too.

—*David Roper*

"Heaven will be the answer to our deepest longings." —David Jeremiah

A MASSIVE CELEBRATION

Read: Revelation 5:6-14

Worship the LORD in the splendor of his holiness; tremble before him, all the earth. —PSALM 96:9

We all love to have someone tell us, "Hey, great job. I appreciate you." And if several people tell us we are doing something right, that's even better.

God loves the praise of His people too, and He truly deserves it. Our most important work on earth is to exalt Him (Psalm 96:9), "that in all things God may be praised through Jesus Christ" (1 Peter 4:11). It's our responsibility and privilege to worship, love, exalt, and serve the Lord.

Revelation 5:9–13 tells of a future day in heaven when believers from "every tribe and language and people and nation" who have been redeemed by Jesus's blood will surround His throne with praises. All of those individuals—multiplied over the millennia—add up to a mind-boggling congregation of God-glorifying people.

God's greatness is so overwhelming, so unfathomable, and so indescribable that millions and millions of people—all praising Him and bowing before Him in worship—will give Him the glory He deserves.

Even now, each of us can participate in celebrating God's majesty by glorifying Him with our lives. And one day we will join with people from every nation in that massive heavenly celebration.

—Dave Branon

"Heaven is a place of unparalleled and indescribable joy." –John Piper

RESERVED FOR YOU

Read: 1 Peter 1:3-9

*In all this you greatly rejoice, though now for a little while you may have
had to suffer grief in all kinds of trials.* —1 PETER 1:6

Have you ever taken one of *those* vacations? You planned to
arrive at a distant location where you knew you'd have a great
time, but on the way you had so many traveling difficulties
that you wondered if the journey was worth it.

Car problems. Traffic delays. Getting lost. Sick kids. Irritable
fellow travelers. You knew the destination would be great,
but the trip was anything but smooth. Yet you kept pressing on
because you knew it would be worth the trouble.

That's a picture of the Christian life. Those who have
trusted Jesus as Savior are on a journey filled with difficulties,
setbacks, tragedies, and obstacles. Trouble always seems to be
present or just around the corner. Yet we know that an indescribably
great destination is in our future (1 Peter 1:4). And
sometimes the assurance of what's reserved for us in heaven is
all that keeps us going.

Peter understood. He said that as we make our way through
life, we will suffer grief as a result of our troubles. Yet we can
actually rejoice through our difficulties, because God has
reserved something special for us at the end of the journey.

Troubled today? Look ahead. Heaven will be worth the trip.

—*Dave Branon*

"Every moment of eternity will be an adventure of discovery." —Ray Stedman

FORETASTES OF
THE KINGDOM

READ: Mark 1:9-15

Jesus went into Galilee, proclaiming the good news of God.
"The time has come," he said. "The kingdom of God has come near.
Repent and believe the good news!" —MARK 1:14–15

When I was ten years old, Baskin-Robbins opened an ice cream store in my neighborhood and encouraged customers to sample ice cream flavors using its iconic pink taste-testing spoons. These provided small but yummy samples of what was to come for those who ordered a full scoop. I took full advantage of the samples!

In her book *Kingdom Calling*, Amy Sherman tells of a pastor who held up one of those pink tasting spoons as he was teaching about joining Jesus in His "grand, sweeping work of restoration." Just as pink spoons offered "foretastes" of the ice cream to come, he encouraged his Christian audience to think of themselves as offering "foretastes" of God's coming kingdom to their "neighbors near and far."

King Jesus taught that the kingdom of God has already arrived in our world through Him (Mark 1:14–15). But it won't fully come until He returns to the world, sits on the throne, and renews all things (Revelation 21:5).

Until Jesus returns, our mission is to partner with Him in giving foretastes—previews—of God's kingdom. One day that kingdom will fully come to earth as it is in heaven. As we wait and anticipate, we too can bring great joy to God the Father. Let's spread His good news today!

—*Jeff Olson*

"Taste and see that the LORD is good; blessed is the one who takes refuge in him." –David, Psalm 34:8

ASCENDED!

Read: 2 Corinthians 5:1-8

We are confident, I say, and would prefer to be away from the body and at home with the Lord. —2 CORINTHIANS 5:8

Joseph Parker (1830–1902) was a beloved English preacher. When his wife Emma died, he didn't have the customary wording inscribed on her gravestone. Instead of the word *died* followed by the date of her death, he chose the word *ascended*.

Parker found great comfort in being reminded that though his wife's body had been placed in the grave, she had been transported to heaven and into the presence of her Savior. When Parker himself died, his friends made sure that his gravestone read:

Ascended November 28, 1902

When a believing loved one dies, or when we ourselves face the process of dying, there's great comfort in the fact that "to be away from the body" is to be "at home with the Lord" (2 Corinthians 5:8).

Death for us is not a dark journey into the unknown. It is not a lonely walk into a strange and friendless place. Rather, it is a glorious transition from the trials of earth into the joys of heaven, where we will be reunited with our loved ones in Christ who have gone before. Best of all, we will enjoy the presence of our Lord.

Yes, when a believer dies, the body is buried but not the soul. It has ascended!

—*Richard DeHaan*

"We must not confuse the present *intermediate* state of our departed Christian loved ones with their yet-future *ultimate* state after the second coming of Christ." —J. Sidlow Baxter, *The Other Side of Death*

HEADLINE EVENT

Read: John 13:33-14:3

"Look, he is coming with the clouds," and "every eye will see him."
—REVELATION 1:7

Did you know that the largest type used by most newspapers for headlines of astounding events has been called "second coming" type? These heavy, black letters are reserved for only the most amazing front-page news stories. This dramatic type has been used to announce the beginning and end of wars, moon landings, presidential election winners, natural disasters, and other significant events.

One day, humankind will witness the great event for which the "second coming" type was named—the return of Jesus Christ. And what a day that will be! The One who ascended to heaven long ago will return to this earth. When our Lord comes back, it will be such a phenomenal occurrence that it will command worldwide attention.

On the day Jesus told His disciples that He would be leaving them, Peter was filled with questions (John 13:36–37). Jesus didn't explain when He would return, but He reassured His disciples that He was going to prepare a place for them and one day "come back" (14:2–3).

When the Savior comes back, His return will command the attention of all earth's inhabitants. It will be a headline event!
—*David Egner*

"The second coming of Christ shall be utterly unlike the first. He came the first time in weakness, a tender infant, born of a poor woman in the manger at Bethlehem, unnoticed, unhonored, and scarcely known. He shall come the second time in royal dignity, with the armies of heaven around Him." —J. C. Ryle

A GOOD WILL

Read: 1 Peter 1:3-12

In [God's] great mercy he has given us new birth into a living hope through the resurrection of Jesus Christ from the dead. —1 PETER 1:3

Perhaps you know someone who didn't receive the inheritance intended by a parent because of a faulty will. In a newspaper column titled "Money & the Law," attorney Jim Flynn says that if you want your estate to go to your chosen recipients instead of to members of the legal profession, you should avoid do-it-yourself wills. Such documents are usually legal, but they are often unclear and fail to make provisions for unforeseen situations. Flynn advises having a formal will to be sure your wishes are carried out.

Man-made wills can fail, but there is no ambiguous language about the inheritance God has in store for us. The apostle Peter affirmed that God "has given us new birth into a living hope through the resurrection of Jesus Christ from the dead, and into an inheritance that can never perish, spoil or fade. This inheritance is kept in heaven for you" (1 Peter 1:3–4).

No fluctuation in the economy can reduce this inheritance. It is not subject to review by the courts nor to debate by squabbling families. No amount of suffering or trials can diminish or change what God has in store for us. Our inheritance is certain and eternal (Hebrews 9:15). And as we live for Him, we are assured that His will for our lives today is "good, pleasing and perfect" (Romans 12:2).

—David McCasland

"God promises us a home that will not be destroyed, a kingdom that will not fade, a city with unshakable foundations, an incorruptible inheritance." —Randy Alcorn, *Heaven*

PULLED IN TWO DIRECTIONS

Read: Philippians 1:19-26

For to me, to live is Christ and to die is gain. —PHILIPPIANS 1:21

As Christians, we all want to go to heaven, but we are pulled in two directions because this life also holds great appeal. We are like the youngster in Sunday school who listened intently while the teacher told about the beauties of heaven. She concluded by saying, "All who are glad you are going to heaven raise your hands." Every hand shot up immediately — except one. "Why don't you want to go to heaven, Johnny?" "Well," he replied, "when I left home, Mom was baking an apple pie."

Now, we shouldn't feel guilty for having a strong desire to enjoy life with all its goodness. Marriage, a family, a fulfilling job, travel, recreation —these all have a legitimate pull. But if the delights of our earthly home are so attractive that we lose sight of God's purpose for putting us here, something's wrong.

The apostle Paul had mixed feelings too. Although he believed he would be released from prison, he also knew that he could fall victim to Nero's sword. This created a conflict. He longed to be with Christ, for that would be "better by far" than anything this world held for him. But he also wanted to live. Not merely to enjoy life but because he was needed (Philippians 1:24).

Paul was pulled in two directions, and in both cases it was for the highest reason. Are we?

—Dennis DeHaan

"God will see to it that the man who finds God in his earthly happiness and thanks him for it does not lack reminder that earthly things are transient, that it is good for him to attune his heart to what is eternal, and that sooner or later there will be times when he can say in all sincerity, 'I wish I were home.'"

—Dietrich Bonhoeffer,
Letters and Papers from Prison

𝝬

OUR HOME IS AHEAD

Read: Hebrews 11:8-10

By faith [Abraham] made his home in the promised land like a stranger in a foreign country. —HEBREWS 11:9

Now that I'm getting closer to the end of life's journey, I'm thinking more like a transient. I suppose it's natural. Abraham first described himself as "a foreigner and stranger" when he was buying a burial plot for Sarah (Genesis 23:4). Time and death make you think about such things.

Most elderly believers say the same thing: There's no home for us this side of heaven. Like the character Pilgrim in John Bunyan's *The Pilgrim's Progress*, once we've caught sight of the Celestial City we can never be content with anything less. Like Abraham, we look for a city whose builder is God (Hebrews 11:10).

In Tolkien's *Lord of the Rings*, as Frodo and the other hobbits set out on their great adventure, they sing, "Home is behind, the world ahead." But for Christians, it's the other way around: The world is behind; our home is ahead.

There are no valleys of weeping there, for "[God] will wipe every tear from [our] eyes. There will be no more death or mourning or crying or pain, for the old order of things has passed away" (Revelation 21:4). That promise makes the present journey easier to endure.

Put another way, it's the hope of going home that keeps me going. I can hardly wait to get there!

—*David Roper*

"How heaven ought to draw on our hearts and lift us above earth! How it should fill our thoughts and brighten our hopes!" —E. M. Bounds

WHAT WILL WE DO IN HEAVEN?

Read: Revelation 22:1-5

His servants will serve him. They will see his face, and his name will be on their foreheads. —REVELATION 22:3-4

I'm sometimes asked what we'll do in heaven and the new earth. Will we sit on clouds and strum celestial harps? Will we flit about on gossamer wings? In his vision, John the apostle saw three future activities.

The first one is serving (Revelation 22:3). Perhaps we'll explore an unknown corner of the universe, or, as C. S. Lewis suggests, govern a distant star. Whatever that service may entail, there will be no sense of inadequacy, no weakness, no weariness. In heaven we'll have minds and bodies equal to the task to which we're assigned.

The second activity is seeing: We "will see his face" (v. 4). "Now we see only a reflection as in a mirror" (1 Corinthians 13:12), but then we shall see our Savior face to face, and we "shall be like Him" (1 John 3:2). This is what Revelation 22:4 means when it says, "his name will be on their foreheads." The name of God represents His perfect character, so to bear His name means to be like Him. We will never again struggle with sin but will reflect the beauty of His holiness forever.

Finally, there is *reigning*. We shall serve our King by ruling and reigning with Him "for ever and ever" (v. 5).

What will we do when we die? We'll serve God, see our Savior, and reign with Him forever. We'll be busy!

—*David Roper*

"What can this incessant craving, and this impotence of attainment mean, unless there was once a happiness belonging to man, of which only the faintest traces remain, in that void which he attempts to fill with everything within his reach?" —Blaise Pascal

BEFORE THEIR TIME

Read: Genesis 2:1-17

The LORD God commanded the man, "You are free to eat from any tree in the garden; but you must not eat from the tree of the knowledge of good and evil, for when you eat from it you will certainly die."
—GENESIS 2:16–17

Last year I said goodbye to a friend from my high school years. David, who struggled with physical challenges his entire life, was just fifty years old when kidney failure took him.

Why do some people die seemingly before their time? Why do parents have to bury their children? These are burning, universal questions, and every last one of us looks for an explanation.

Thankfully, the Bible doesn't leave us in the dark. Genesis reveals that human beings once lived in a perfect world, with no death or fear. All that God originally created was "very good" (Genesis 1:31). That is, until evil and sin entered the world and caused all of creation to enter a state of perpetual brokenness. Ever since then, life in this world has been far from perfect. That's why people, like my friend David, die.

As C. S. Lewis said in *The Weight of Glory,* in every person there is an "inconsolable longing" for a better world, free of sickness and death. For believers in Jesus, that world is coming. Through Him, God will one day fully restore the world to the way it was intended to be (Revelation 21:5).

Lewis went on to say, "At present we are on the outside of the world, the wrong side of the door . . . but all the leaves of the New Testament are rustling with the rumor that it will not always be so. Someday, God willing, we shall get in."

—*Jeff Olson*

"The resurrection of the body . . . declares that God will make good and bring to perfection the human project he started in the Garden of Eden." —Timothy George

IN HIS PRESENCE

Read: 1 Corinthians 15:50-58

Death has been swallowed up in victory. —1 CORINTHIANS 15:54

As the congregation around me sang the final verse of "Amazing Grace," I couldn't sing. I found myself instead wiping tears from my eyes as I stared at John Newton's words, "When we've been there ten thousand years, . . . we've no less days to sing God's praise than when we'd first begun."

At that moment I wasn't interested in ten thousand years in heaven. All I could think of was that my daughter was already there. Melissa, who just a few months earlier had been looking forward to her senior year of high school, was in heaven. She was already experiencing an eternity that we can only talk and sing about.

When Melissa was killed in a car accident in the spring of 2002, heaven took on new meaning for our family. Because our bright, beautiful teen had trusted Jesus Christ as her Savior, we knew she was there. As Paul said, "Death has been swallowed up in victory" (1 Corinthians 15:54). To us, heaven became even more real. We knew that as we talked with God, we were talking to Someone who had our Melissa in His presence.

The reality of heaven is one of the Bible's most glorious truths. It's a real place where our loved ones live in the presence of our great God, forever serving Him and singing His praises—all because of His amazing grace!

—*Dave Branon*

"Every saint in heaven is as a flower in the garden of God." —Jonathan Edwards

FIRST SIGHT

Read: John 13:36-14:3

They will see his face, and his name will be on their foreheads.
—REVELATION 22:4

When I was flying from Chicago to Tampa, I noticed a family on the plane. And from the excitement of the two children, I assumed they had never been to Florida. As we neared our destination, clouds blocked our view of the ground. Only when we began our descent did the plane finally break through the clouds.

At the first sight of the land below, the mother exclaimed to the two little ones beside her, "Look, that must be Florida!" After a few moments of silence, the young boy said, "But Mom, where are the palm trees? I can't see them!" His idea of Florida immediately brought to his mind those tropical trees, and he expected to see them first.

Christian, as you anticipate the day you will arrive in heaven, what do you want to see first? It will certainly be wonderful to greet our loved ones who have gone before. My, what a thrill to visit with the believers of the past, and how exciting to see the glorious sights of heaven! And yet, as delightful as all of this will be, our greatest joy will be to see the Lord Jesus himself—for He is the One who made it possible for us to go there.

Yes, in the words of the old hymn, "I long to meet my Savior first of all."

—*Richard DeHaan*

"Jesus is the joy and glory of heaven."

—E. M. Bounds

✕

WHO'S GOING TO HEAVEN?

Read: Romans 3:21–28

For we maintain that a person is justified by faith apart from the works of the law. —ROMANS 3:28

A poll for *U.S. News & World Report* asked one thousand adults their opinion about who would likely make it into heaven. At the top of that list, to no one's surprise, was a well-known religious figure. Several celebrities were also listed. But it was surprising to me that of the people being surveyed, 87 percent thought they themselves were likely to get into heaven.

I can't help but wonder what qualifications for admission into heaven they had in mind. People have many erroneous ideas about what God requires.

Is it virtuous character? Giving generous contributions to deserving charities? Following an orthodox creed? Attending church and being involved in religious activities? Commendable as these qualities may be, they miss by an eternity the one thing God requires for entrance into heaven—personal faith in Jesus Christ as Savior and Lord (John 1:12; 1 Timothy 2:5). Although commitment in Jesus will no doubt be seen in a person's actions (James 2:14–20), charitable giving or religious activity is not a substitute for trusting in Jesus's sacrificial death for our sin.

Are you confident that you're headed for heaven? You can be if you trust in Jesus.

—Vernon Grounds

———

"What! Get to heaven on your own strength? Why, you might as well try to climb to the moon on a rope of sand." —George Whitefield

PRAISEWORTHY

Read: Revelation 5

I heard the voice of many angels around the throne.
—REVELATION 5:11 (NKJV)

The Grand Rapids Symphony Orchestra and Symphonic Choir were presenting their annual Christmas concert. Near the conclusion, the four thousand members of the audience joined them in singing, "Joy to the world, the Lord is come! Let earth receive her King." I got chills when we sang the words, "And heaven and nature sing."

Despite the magnificence of that moment, it was but a faint shadow of the praise that will be raised to the Lamb in heaven. Jesus is worthy of the adoration and praise of all beings: "Worthy is the Lamb, who was slain, to receive power and wealth and wisdom and strength and honor and glory and praise!" (Revelation 5:12).

In Revelation 5, we read John's description of a widening circle of praise to the Lord. It begins with "four living creatures and the twenty-four elders" (v. 8). They are joined by angels numbering "ten thousand times ten thousand" (v. 11).

But that's not all. Every creature in heaven, on earth, and in the sea will one day sing, "To him who sits on the throne and to the Lamb be praise and honor and glory and power, for ever and ever!" (v. 13).

We don't have to wait for that day to sing praise to the Lamb. He is worthy of our praise right now!

—David Egner

"Music is God's gift to man, the only art of heaven given to earth—the only art of earth we take to heaven." —Walter Savage Landor

"THE BEST IS YET TO BE"

Read: Romans 8:25-39

I am convinced that neither death nor life . . . will be able to separate us from the love of God. —ROMANS 8:38–39

Oswald Chambers loved the poetry of Robert Browning and often quoted a phrase from the poem "Rabbi Ben Ezra": "The best is yet to be, the last of life, for which the first was made: Our times are in His hand."

As principal of the Bible Training College in London from 1911 to 1915, Chambers often said that the school's initials, B.T.C., also stood for "Better To Come." He believed that the future was always bright with possibility because of Christ. In a letter to former students written during the dark days of World War I, Chambers said, "Whatever transpires, it is ever 'the best is yet to be.' "

For the Christian, this is certainly true when we think about going to heaven. But can we believe that our remaining days on earth will be better than the past? If our hope is centered in Christ, the answer is a resounding yes!

The apostle Paul concluded the stirring eighth chapter of Romans with the assurance that nothing in the present or the future can separate us from the love of God, which is in Christ Jesus our Lord (vv. 38–39). Because we are held in the relentless grip of God's unchanging love, we can experience deeper fellowship with Him, no matter what difficulties come our way.

In Christ, "the best is yet to be."

—*David McCasland*

———

"If you are a Christian, you are not a citizen of this world trying to get to heaven; you are a citizen of heaven making your way through this world." –Vance Havner

WE'LL SING AND SHOUT!

Read: Revelation 19:6-8

Those who have leprosy are cleansed, the deaf hear.
—MATTHEW 11:5

I was enjoying a concert by a singing group when I noticed what was happening in the front rows of the auditorium. A sign-language interpreter was gracefully communicating the words of each song to about twenty-five people who were deaf.

When the vocalists sang "Victory in Jesus," the man who was both the pianist and emcee asked the translator if her group would "sing" the chorus. She agreed, and he began to play. No voices were heard, but we sat in awe as her group joyfully expressed the words with their hands. Their faces beamed, reflecting the meaning of each phrase.

I glanced at the five vocalists on the stage. Their faces were fixed intently on that group of twenty-five as they "sang" the marvelous lyrics to that song. It was a thrilling experience.

I couldn't help but think of what it will be like in heaven. The hearing impaired will be able to hear and sing. They will be part of the vast chorus of the redeemed as they join the angels in proclaiming the praises of the Most High God and of the Lamb.

A day of rejoicing awaits every believer in Jesus Christ. We'll all be transformed, glorified, made whole. When we all get to heaven, we will sing and we will shout about our victory in Jesus.

—*David Egner*

"Music is transcendent—a bridge between this world and another. . . . In heaven God will unleash our creativity, not confine it." — Randy Alcorn, *Heaven*

KEEP ETERNITY IN MIND

Read: Ecclesiastes 5:18-20

Command them to do good, to be rich in good deeds, and to be generous and willing to share. In this way they will lay up treasure for themselves as a firm foundation for the coming age. —1 TIMOTHY 6:18–19

Many years ago a group of people mistakenly thought they could best prepare for eternity by taking no pleasure in life here on earth. They ate the simplest food, lived in solitude, never bathed, and wore a camel skin garment with the hair on the inside to produce itching.

Today some Christians err by going to the opposite extreme. They get so caught up in the pleasures and comforts of this life that they give little thought to the life hereafter.

The writer of Ecclesiastes knew the right balance. He said it is "appropriate" to enjoy our earthly blessings (Ecclesiastes 5:18). He also reminded us that whatever degree of health and wealth we possess is "a gift of God" (v. 19). When we keep in mind the source of all our good, we are bound to think of God and of eternity. This should not make us morbid, but it should fill us with such gladness that the thought of dying won't disturb us as much (v. 20).

Christians are citizens of two worlds. God desires that the earthly blessings He gives us contribute to our happiness. But He warns us not to set our hearts on them. Paul said that by doing good we can store up riches for our eternal future (1 Timothy 6:17–19).

We can best enjoy God's earthly blessings when we keep eternity and heaven in mind.

—Herb Vander Lugt

"Heaven's riches are rooted in heaven's God." —Randy Alcorn, *Heaven*

✕

TO DIE IS GAIN

Read: Revelation 21:1-7

To me, to live is Christ and to die is gain. —PHILIPPIANS 1:21

Not long ago I was feeling gratitude to God for His goodness to me during the past eighty years. But as I reflected on my life, I felt grief as I recalled the day when I learned that my brother Cornelius had been killed in action during World War II. He was only twenty. Unlike me, he never realized the aspirations and hopes that are part of youth. Neither did the many young people who died during the years I was a pastor. Every one of these experiences was emotionally and spiritually draining. Such grief and loss!

C. S. Lewis reminds us that death and grief are not the whole picture, however. At the close of his book *The Last Battle,* Peter, Edmund, and Lucy meet the great lion Aslan (a symbol of Christ in heaven), who tells them that they died in an accident. Lewis wrote, "And as He spoke, He no longer looked to them like a lion; but the things that began to happen after that were so great and beautiful that I cannot write them. And for us this is the end of all the stories. . . . But for them it is only the beginning of the real story."

For the Christian, the real story is endless life and joy with Jesus! "To live is Christ," which means joyful service, as well as suffering and grief. But "to die is gain" (Philippians 1:21). Then, the real story begins.

—Herb Vander Lugt

"Jesus did not die on the cross for people's sin so that we would believe in heaven—but that we would believe in *Him*."
—Billy Graham

READY TO GO HOME

Read: 2 Timothy 4:6-8, 16-18

*I am already being poured out like a drink offering, and the time
for my departure is near.* —2 TIMOTHY 4:6

Because I have traveled widely in my ministry, I've had to
spend a lot of time away from home. Although some hotels
promise to make me "feel at home," few of them achieve it. In
fact, some make me wish fervently that I *were* at home!

During his final days on earth, the apostle Paul had a deep
longing for his heavenly home. His thoughts turned toward
the warm welcome he would receive from the Lord, "the righteous Judge" (2 Timothy 4:8). Although he was facing death,
thoughts of heaven kept his spirit hopeful.

This reminds me of an old man and his grandson who were
sitting on a dock late one afternoon. The two chatted about
everything, it seemed—why water is wet, why seasons change,
why girls hate worms, what life is like. Finally the boy looked
up and asked, "Grandpa, does anybody ever see God?" "Son,"
said the old man as he looked across the still waters of the lake,
"it's getting so now I hardly see anything else."

Aging should be like that. Praying should come more easily.
Communion with the Father in heaven should be as natural
as breathing. Thoughts of seeing Jesus and going home should
increasingly occupy our minds. That's how we'll know we're
ready to go home.

—*Haddon Robinson*

"Like Adam, we have all lost Paradise; and yet we carry Paradise
around inside of us in the form of a longing for, almost a memory
of, a blessedness that is no more, or the dream of blessedness that
may someday be again." –Frederick Buechner, *The Magnificent
Defeat*

GOING FOR THE GOLD

Read: Revelation 21:1-3; 15-27

The great street of the city was of gold, as pure as transparent glass.
—REVELATION 21:21

This may come as a surprise, but the city of gold in today's world is New York. Beneath the frantic streets of the Big Apple lies the world's largest cache of gold. Eighty feet under the business district is a vault that contains about one-fourth of the world's monetary gold reserves.

As might be expected, security is airtight. The vault has no doors, only a narrow passageway that is closed by a rotating steel cylinder. Elaborate precautions ensure that no unauthorized entry is ever made into the vault.

The thought of so much gold in one place is exciting—yet it belongs to someone else.

Contrast that picture of gold, safely stored away and protected by technology and man's best efforts, with the gold that's out in the open in heaven. While the gold in New York is inaccessible to all but a privileged few, heaven's gold is so plentiful that it is used to pave the streets. But far better than being near gold is that we will be near our Lord and Savior.

To get to that golden city, you have to admit your sin and trust Jesus Christ as the One who died to pay the penalty for it. Don't let anything stop you from going for something far more valuable than gold—the joy of being with God forever.

—*Dave Branon*

"The heart that indulges itself in great earthly loves will have less for heaven." —E. M. Bounds

ASTONISHED JOY

Read: Philippians 3:20-41

They will see his face. —REVELATION 22:4

Do you sometimes wonder what heaven will be like? All of us do, I suppose. I confess, however, that the nearer I come to the end of earth's journey the more often I indulge in "sanctified curiosity" about the home Jesus has promised to believers. What will be my reaction when I cross the river and enter into glory?

British theologian Stephen Neill asked himself the same question. At first he was inclined to think his emotion would be astonishment. But then he decided that his emotion, "to put it a little more precisely," would be "astonished joy."

Yes, astonished joy indeed! The apostle Paul called believers in Christ citizens of heaven, and he wrote, "We eagerly await a Savior . . . who . . . will transform our lowly bodies so that they will be like his glorious body" (Philippians 3:20–21). Paul looked forward to a day when sin and pain and grief would be gone forever.

What a soul-thrilling vision that will be when we see our Lord! What indescribable ecstasy we will experience! Fully aware at last of the sheer marvel of redemptive grace that has brought us into the presence of unparalleled beauty, we will be filled with *astonished joy*.

—*Vernon Grounds*

"Heaven will prove the consummate flower and fruit of the whole creation and of all the history of the universe." —A. A. Hodge

NO JOKE

Read: John 14:1-6

I will come back and take you to be with me that you also may be where I am. —JOHN 14:3

I have heard that humor is sometimes used to deal with important things we don't really understand. If that's true, I can see why there are so many jokes about heaven.

We understand so little about what life is like for those who are "with the Lord." When we lose a loved one, we struggle to grasp why God "needed" that person more than we did. Because justice and reward are so imperfect on earth, it seems hard to imagine a place where God perfectly administers both. So we chuckle at stories about someone "who died and knocked on the pearly gates."

Even the most knowledgeable theologian knows little of that marvelous place the Bible calls heaven. Jesus didn't give a detailed description of life after death, but He promised His followers a home with Him. He said, "If I go and prepare a place for you, I will come back and take you to be with me that you also may be where I am" (John 14:3).

We don't understand everything about heaven, but we believe our Savior's promise. By faith in the integrity and power of the One who has spoken, we accept what we cannot fully comprehend. We live with hope and assurance of all that He has in store for us. And that's no joke.

—*David McCasland*

"There is a land of pure delight, where saints immortal reign; infinite day excludes the night, and pleasures banish pain." —Isaac Watts

X

THE MUSIC OF HEAVEN

Read: Revelation 5

They sang a new song, saying: "You are worthy to take the scroll and to open its seals." —REVELATION 5:9

A great celebration was staged in Boston in 1869 to commemorate the end of the American Civil War. A man who was there wrote a letter to a friend and described some of the events.

He told of a ten thousand–voice choir supported by a thousand-piece orchestra. The violin section included two hundred musicians, led by the world's greatest violinist, Ole Bull. Two hundred anvils were used in the Anvil Chorus. And when the soloist sang "The Star Spangled Banner" and hit high C with the full orchestra and chorus, her voice was so loud and clear that it seemed to soar above everything else.

With those memories flooding his mind, the letter writer concluded, "I am an old man now, but I am looking forward to the music of heaven—music infinitely superior to the marvelous chorus I listened to that day."

Yes, as thrilling as that music was, who can imagine the sound in heaven when "thousands upon thousands, and ten thousand times ten thousand" join in praise to our Lord! (Revelation 5:11).

I too am looking forward to hearing the heavenly choirs as they exalt Christ. And I'll be adding my voice to theirs. I may not qualify to sing in any choir here. But just wait till you hear me there!

—*Richard DeHaan*

"Reflect how very captivating, soothing, and enlivening is music. The ear revels in it. . . . What, then, must heavenly harmony be, if our imperfect music is so delightful?" —Father J. Boudreau, *The Happiness of Heaven*

THINKING ABOUT HEAVEN

Read: Psalm 16

You make known to me the path of life; you will fill me with joy in your presence, with eternal pleasures at your right hand. —PSALM 16:11

In his classic devotional book titled *The Saints' Everlasting Rest*, English Puritan pastor and author Richard Baxter (1615–1691) wrote:

"Why are not our hearts continually set on heaven? Why dwell we not there in constant contemplation? . . . Bend thy soul to study eternity, busy thyself about the life to come, habituate thyself to such contemplations, and let not those thoughts be seldom and cursory, but bathe thyself in heaven's delights."

That's sound advice. Instead of spending all of our time thinking about where we are, we as believers in Jesus Christ also need to think about where we're going to be. We'll go to a place prepared especially for us (John 14:2). We'll be with God, where we'll enjoy "eternal pleasures" (Psalm 16:11).

Baxter goes on to point out four benefits of thinking about heaven: It protects us from temptation because it keeps the heart focused on what pleases God. It maintains the vigor of the Christian life. It provides medicine for our afflictions, cheering our spirits and easing our suffering. And it makes us an encouragement to our fellow pilgrims.

With this in mind, we ask as Baxter did, "Why are not our hearts continually set on heaven?"

—*David Egner*

"There have been times when I think we do not desire heaven but more often I find myself wondering whether, in our heart of hearts, we have ever desired anything else." —C. S. Lewis

LAND OF THE LIVING

Read: 2 Corinthians 5:1-9

For we live by faith, not by sight. —2 CORINTHIANS 5:7

My favorite gospel-sharing article is called "When I Think of Heaven." It's written by Joni Eareckson Tada, who is paralyzed from her neck down because of a diving accident during her teenage years. Joni admits that thinking about heaven isn't always easy, especially since we have to die to get there, unless Jesus returns first! Yet God works through trials to help us focus our minds on heaven.

As one who lives, travels, and ministers in a wheelchair, Joni writes confidently about heaven: "There's not a doubt in my mind that I'll be fantastically more excited and ready for it than if I were on my feet. You see, suffering gets us ready for heaven. Heaven becomes our passion."

The apostle Paul knew that kind of passion. We groan for heaven, he said, not because we long to die, but because we long to really live, to be with our Lord forever (2 Corinthians 5:6–8). But until then, "we live by faith, not by sight" (v. 7).

I heard about an elderly gentleman who was greeted in this way: "Nice to see you in the land of the living!" "Oh, I'm not in the land of the living," he replied. "I'm in the land of the dying. But I look forward to being in the land of the living soon when I'm in heaven." That man's heart is already there! Can that be said of us?

—*Joanie Yoder*

"I haven't been cheated out of being a complete person—I'm just going through a forty-year delay, and God is with me even through that. Being 'glorified'—I know the meaning of that now. It's the time, after my death here, when I'll be on my feet dancing."
—Joni Eareckson Tada

JOY ON THE JOURNEY

Read: Psalm 145

The Lord is good to all; he has compassion on all he has made.
—PSALM 145:9

What the evangelist said shocked many in his audience: "Heaven is my home, but I'm not homesick." He wasn't downplaying the anticipation we should have for heaven. He was reflecting the truth that our heavenly Father wants us to enjoy with gratitude the good things He has provided for us in this world. This old Jewish proverb reinforces the idea: "In the judgment, a man will be held accountable for every blessing he refused to enjoy."

For those who are near the end of life, are lonely or depressed, or whose bodies are weak and disease-ravaged, it is understandable that they long for the indescribable blessings of the land of no more heartache, pain, and tears. But as Christians, we certainly must not disregard the daily mercies and the rich abundance our Father gives to us. The Bible says that God "richly provides us with everything for our enjoyment" (1 Timothy 6:17). His goodness is shown to all humankind in "rain from heaven and crops in their seasons; he provides you with plenty of food and fills your hearts with joy" (Acts 14:17). In other words, all of us, even non-Christians, are able to enjoy much of life's goodness.

Yes, heaven awaits us, but God wants us to be glad and enjoy all His goodness as we journey homeward.

—*Vernon Grounds*

———

"How priceless is your unfailing love, O God! People take refuge in the shadow of your wings. They feast on the abundance of your house; you give them drink from your river of delights." —David, Psalm 36:7-9

THE BOOK OF NAMES

Read: Revelation 20:11-15

Another book was opened, which is the book of life.
—REVELATION 20:12

Late one afternoon in nineteenth-century London, two sight-seeing soldiers went to visit the magnificent Westminster Abbey but found its doors locked. Arthur Stanley, who had become dean of the Abbey in 1863, was walking outside at the time and noticed them. When he learned that they couldn't return the next day, he unlocked the door and gave them a personal tour.

As they walked through that awe-inspiring building, Stanley talked about the honor of being immortalized by having one's name inscribed on a monument inside. Then he added, "You may have a more enduring monument than this, for this building will molder into dust and be forgotten, but you, if your names are written in the Lamb's book of life, will abide forever." Before parting, he urged them to receive Christ as their Savior. "If we never meet on earth again," he said, "we will certainly meet in heaven." That day they decided to trust Christ.

When you accept Jesus as your Savior, your name will be immortalized on the pages of the Lamb's book of life too.

—*Vernon Grounds*

"Is my name written there, on the page white and fair? In the book of your kingdom, is my name written there?"

—Mary Kidder

𝄢

HEAVEN'S SURPRISES

Read: Revelation 22:1–5

Christ Jesus came into the world to save sinners—of whom I am the worst.
—1 TIMOTHY 1:15

Scripture gives us only a glimpse of the glory we will share in heaven with our crucified and risen Savior. Just think—no more sorrow, no more death, no more crying, no more pain, for the former things will have passed away! (Revelation 21:4).

These brief glimpses make us eager to know more of what will flood us with awe when we get there. No doubt the dwelling place of the Lord will be infinitely more beautiful and breathtaking than we are capable of imagining.

Among the surprises that await us in heaven will be three astonishing ones that John Newton pointed out. The converted slave-dealer, who wrote the hymn "Amazing Grace," perceptively foresaw what every sinner will feel who has been redeemed by Christ's atoning sacrifice. He wrote, "If I ever reach heaven, I expect to find three wonders there: First, to meet some I had not thought to see there; second, to miss some I had thought to meet there; and third, the greatest wonder of all, to find myself there!" And that greatest wonder will cause John Newton and all of God's children to fall on their knees in gratitude for God's amazing grace. But let's not wait. Now is the time to begin expressing our gratitude.

—*Vernon Grounds*

"One of the most staggering truths of the Scriptures is to understand that we do not earn our way to heaven." —Ravi Zacharias

DEAD COMING BACK TO LIFE

Read: Genesis 9:1-17

Swarms of living creatures will live wherever the river flows.
There will be large numbers of fish, because this water flows there and
makes the salt water fresh; so where the river flows everything will live.
—EZEKIEL 47:9

The Dead Sea in Israel is a one-of-a-kind place to take a dip. Tourists who enter its waters immediately realize that swimming aids aren't necessary. Due to its exceptionally high concentration of salt, people simply float on its surface like apples bobbing in a barrel of water.

The Dead Sea is also the lowest land-based point on earth. The Jordan River empties into it, but nothing flows out of it. And due to its toxic blend of minerals, nothing lives in it. But one day the Dead Sea will undergo a radical change.

The last book of the Bible reports that once Jesus returns, God will send the "Holy City, the new Jerusalem" down to earth from heaven (Revelation 21:2). The Old Testament prophet Ezekiel received a vision of the temple area in the new Jerusalem. He saw a river flowing from the temple toward the Dead Sea. Ezekiel was told that the waters from the river "will make the salty waters of the Dead Sea fresh and pure. . . . Fish will abound in the Dead Sea, for its waters will become fresh. Life will flourish wherever this water flows" (Ezekiel 47:8–10 NLT).

Ezekiel's vision is a picture of the great restoration we look forward to—the time when even the deadest parts of Earth will come back to life.

—*Jeff Olson*

"'Dry bones, hear the word of the LORD! This is what the Sovereign LORD says to these bones: I will make breath enter you, and you will come to life. . . . Then you will know that I am the LORD.'"
—Ezekiel 37:4-6

THE OTHER SIDE

Read: Revelation 21

*[God] will wipe every tear from their eyes. . . . The old order
of things has passed away.* —REVELATION 21:4

Many years ago a doctor made a house call on a dying patient, who asked, "Doctor, what will heaven be like?" The physician paused, trying to think of a helpful reply. Just then they heard the sound of scratching on the closed door of the patient's bedroom.

"Do you hear that?" the doctor asked. "It's my dog. I left him downstairs, but he got impatient and came up here looking for me. He doesn't know what's in this room, but he knows his master is here. I believe that's how it is with heaven. We don't know what it's like, but we know that Jesus will be there. And really, nothing else matters."

The Bible gives us a few faith-strengthening glimpses of what life will be like beyond the closed door of death. We know that eternity will be a place of radiant splendor (Revelation 21:23). We know that it will be a place of reunion as we meet again those we have loved and from whom we have been parted for a little while (1 Thessalonians 4:17). We know that there will be "no more death or mourning or crying" (Revelation 21:4).

But above all, when we get to the other side, we will be with Jesus, our Lord and Master, who eagerly awaits us.

—Vernon Grounds

"Heaven would hardly be a place longed for or desired were it not that this is where Christ is." —Wilbur M. Smith, The Biblical Doctrine of Heaven

DOORWAY TO HEAVEN

Read: 2 Corinthians 5:1-8

We are confident, I say, and would prefer to be away from the body and at home with the Lord. —2 CORINTHIANS 5:8

In his book *God Cares for You*, Walter B. Knight gives this account of the memorial service in 1929 for the widely known Bible teacher and author F. B. Meyer:

"London has seldom witnessed a funeral such as was held for him. There was not a single note of grief or tragedy heard. The Scriptures all spoke of the Christian's hope of immortality; and Easter hymns were sung. As the organ began to play at the conclusion of the service, the vast audience rose and stood with bowed heads, waiting for the funeral march to begin. But to their surprise they heard the triumphant notes of the 'Hallelujah Chorus.' What music could have been more appropriate! A faithful soldier of the cross had been ushered into the presence of his King."

Many people are terrified by the thought of dying. It is looked upon as the most tragic of all our human experiences. To be sure, there's pain in being separated from those who are dear to us. The physical discomfort that sometimes accompanies dying is not pleasant to endure. At times our faith may falter as we lose sight of the glory that awaits us. That's why we must never forget that death for the Christian is but the doorway to heaven!

—*Richard DeHaan*

———

"God never said the journey would be easy, but He did say the arrival would be worthwhile." —Max Lucado, *In the Eye of the Storm*

TO BE CONTINUED

Read: Revelation 22:1-5

There will be no more night. They will not need the light of a lamp or the light of the sun, for the Lord God will give them light. And they will reign for ever and ever. —REVELATION 22:5

Imagine yourself seated comfortably in your favorite easy chair, fully absorbed in a magazine article. Your interest increases as you read down the page. Then, just as the story reaches a climax, your eyes come to the words, "To be continued." How disappointing!

Sometimes, however, the words "to be continued" can bring great joy. This is especially true as the Christian contemplates God's blessings. Commenting on this idea, C. H. Spurgeon wrote, "What a comfort to remember that the Lord's mercy and lovingkindness are to be continued! Much as we have experienced in the long years of our pilgrimage, we have by no means outlived eternal love. Providential goodness is an endless chain, a stream which follows the pilgrim, a wheel perpetually revolving, a star forever shining and leading us to the place where He is who was once a babe in Bethlehem. All the volumes which record the doings of divine grace are but part of a series 'to be continued.' "

That's what makes the Christian life so exciting—it's just getting started! God's goodness to us is to be continued. The blessings of redemption are to be continued. Our relationship with the heavenly Father is to be continued. It's comforting to know also that some things—in fact, all that's painful—will be discontinued.

Yes, we'll have an eternity to enjoy the splendors of heaven, for they are all "to be continued"!

—*Richard DeHaan*

"When we've been there ten thousand years, bright shining as the sun, we've no less days to sing God's praise than when we'd first begun." —John Newton

ALL THINGS NEW

Read: Revelation 21:1-8

He who was seated on the throne said, "I am making everything new!"
—REVELATION 21:5

Russian scientists recently discovered plant matter in the burrow of an Ice Age squirrel—stuff that had been frozen for thousands of years. They took the material to their laboratory, where they successfully regenerated a *Silene stenophylla* plant.

What these scientists did for one plant, Jesus will do for the entire planet. Peter declares that one day there will be "the destruction of the heavens by fire, and the elements will melt in the heat" (2 Peter 3:12). But from this stricken world, shaken down to its foundation, Jesus will create "a new heaven and a new earth, where righteousness dwells" (2 Peter 3:13).

When Jesus returns, He will make "everything new" (Revelation 21:5). Notice that Jesus will not make "new everything." He will not brush this world aside and replace it with something else. Rather he will take everything that is already here and make it new.

What Jesus will do for the world He will also do for you. You may bear the scars of having been a sinner living in a broken world—staggering beneath the burden of deep wounds (some self-inflicted and some dealt by others)—but you belong to the "everything" that Jesus will make new. You will rise again, and then "He will wipe every tear from [your] eyes" (Revelation 21:4).

If you put your trust in Jesus, this promise is for you. Lean on Him, and lean into the newness of your future.

—*Mike Wittmer*

——

"Jehovah creates a new heaven and new earth which so fascinate by their splendor, so satisfy every wish, that all remembrance of the first, of wishing them back again, is utterly out of the question." —Frank Delitzsch

OUR DAILY BREAD WRITERS

DAVE BRANON

Senior editor with Discovery House, Dave has been involved with *Our Daily Bread* since the 1980s. He has written several books, including *Beyond the Valley* and *Stand Firm,* both Discovery House publications.

ANNE CETAS

After becoming a Christian in her late teens, Anne was introduced to *Our Daily Bread* right away and began reading it. Now she reads it for a living as an editor of *Our Daily Bread.*

BILL CROWDER

A former pastor who is now senior content advisor for Our Daily Bread Ministries, Bill travels extensively as a Bible conference teacher, sharing God's truths with fellow believers in Malaysia and Singapore and other places where Our Daily Bread Ministries has international offices.

LAWRENCE DARMANI

Lawrence's first novel, *Grief Child,* won the Commonwealth Writers' Prize as best first book from Africa. He is editor of *Step* magazine, and CEO of Step Publishers. He is married and lives in Accra, Ghana, with his family.

DENNIS DEHAAN (1932–2014)

In 1981 Dennis became the second managing editor of *Our Daily Bread,* replacing the original editor, Henry Bosch. A former pastor, he loved preaching and teaching the Word of God.

RICHARD DEHAAN (1923-2002)

Son of the founder of Our Daily Bread Ministries, Dr. M. R. DeHaan, Richard was responsible for the ministry's entrance into television. Under his leadership, *Day of Discovery*, the ministry's long-running TV program, made its debut in 1968.

DAVID EGNER

A retired editor for Our Daily Bread Ministries and longtime *Our Daily Bread* writer, David was also a college professor during his working career. In fact, he was a writing instructor for both Anne Cetas and Julie Ackerman Link at Cornerstone University.

DENNIS FISHER

As a research editor at Our Daily Bread Ministries, Dennis uses his theological training to guarantee biblical accuracy. He is also an expert in C. S. Lewis studies.

VERNON GROUNDS (1914-2010)

A longtime college president (Denver Seminary) and board member for Our Daily Bread Ministries, Vernon's life story was told in the Discovery House book *Transformed by Love*.

CINDY HESS KASPER

An editor for the Our Daily Bread Ministries publication *Our Daily Journey*, Cindy began writing for *Our Daily Bread* in 2006.

ALBERT LEE

For several years, Albert Lee was director of international ministries for Our Daily Bread Ministries while writing for *Our Daily Bread*.

JULIE ACKERMAN LINK (1950–2015)

A book editor by profession, Julie starting writing for *Our Daily Bread* in 2000. Her book *Above All, Love* was published in 2008 by Discovery House.

DAVID MCCASLAND

Living in Colorado, David enjoys the beauty of God's grandeur as displayed in the Rocky Mountains. An accomplished biographer, David has written several books, including *Oswald Chambers: Abandoned to God* and *Eric Liddell: Pure Gold*.

JEFF OLSON

Jeff is a licensed professional counselor and has worked for Our Daily Bread Ministries as a counselor and a writer since 1992. He has authored a number of Discovery Series booklets and writes for *Our Daily Journey*, where the articles in this book first appeared. Jeff and his wife, Diane, have been married since 1986 and have raised two daughters.

HADDON ROBINSON

Haddon has taught hundreds of young preachers the art of preaching. He is former president of Denver Seminary and served for many years as a professor at Gordon-Conwell Theological Seminary.

DAVID ROPER

David Roper lives in Idaho, where he takes advantage of the natural beauty of his state. He has been writing for *Our Daily Bread* since 2000, and he has published several successful books with Discovery House, including *Teach Us to Number Our Days*.

JENNIFER BENSON SCHULDT

Chicagoan Jennifer Schuldt writes from the perspective of a mom of a growing family. She has written for *Our Daily Bread* since 2010, and she also pens articles for another Our Daily Bread Ministries publication: *Our Daily Journey*.

JOE STOWELL

As president of Cornerstone University, Joe stays connected to today's young adults in a leadership role. A popular speaker and a former pastor, Joe has written a number of books over the years, including *Strength for the Journey* and *Jesus Nation*.

HERB VANDER LUGT (1920-2006)

For many years, Herb was the research editor at Our Daily Bread Ministries, responsible for checking the biblical accuracy of the booklets published by the ministry. A World War II veteran, Herb spent several years as a pastor before his Our Daily Bread Ministries tenure began.

PAUL VAN GORDER (1921-2009)

A writer for *Our Daily Bread* in the 1980s and 1990s, Paul was a noted pastor and Bible teacher—both in the Atlanta area where he lived and through the *Day of Discovery* TV program.

SHERIDAN VOYSEY

Sheridan is based in Oxford, England. His books include *Resilient*, *Resurrection Year*, and the award-winning *Unseen Footprints*. He has been featured in numerous TV and radio programs, including *Day of Discovery* and *100 Huntley Street*, is a regular contributor to faith programs on BBC Radio 2, and speaks at conferences and events around the world.

MARVIN WILLIAMS

Marvin's first foray into Our Daily Bread Ministries came as a writer for *Our Daily Journey*. In 2007, he penned his first *Our Daily Bread* article. Marvin is pastor of a church in Lansing, Michigan.

MIKE WITTMER

Dr. Mike Wittmer is professor of systematic and historical theology at Grand Rapids Theological Seminary. He has written several books, including *Heaven Is a Place on Earth*. The articles in this book are adapted from *Our Daily Journey*.

JOANIE YODER (1934-2004)

For ten years, until her death in 2004, Joanie wrote for *Our Daily Bread*. In addition, she published the book *God Alone* with Discovery House.

SCRIPTURE INDEX
OF KEY VERSES

NOTE TO THE READER

The publisher invites you to share your response to the message of this book by writing Discovery House, P.O. Box 3566, Grand Rapids, MI 49501, U.S.A. For information about other Discovery House books, music, or DVDs, contact us at the same address or call 1-800-653-8333. Find us at dhp.org or send e-mail to books@dhp.org.